Samuel French Acting Edition

Songbook

Book and Music by
Monty Norman

Book and Lyrics by
Julian More

Lyrics Copyright © 1981, 1984 by Music Twenty-Eight, Inc.
Book Copyright © 1981, 1985 by Music Twenty-Eight, Inc.
All Rights Reserved

SONGBOOK is fully protected under the copyright laws of the United States of America, the British Commonwealth, including Canada, and all other countries of the Copyright Union. All rights, including professional and amateur stage productions, recitation, lecturing, public reading, motion picture, radio broadcasting, television and the rights of translation into foreign languages are strictly reserved.

ISBN 978-0-573-68162-2

www.SamuelFrench.com
www.SamuelFrench.co.uk

FOR PRODUCTION ENQUIRIES

UNITED STATES AND CANADA
Info@SamuelFrench.com
1-866-598-8449

UNITED KINGDOM AND EUROPE
Plays@SamuelFrench.co.uk
020-7255-4302

Each title is subject to availability from Samuel French, depending upon country of performance. Please be aware that *SONGBOOK* may not be licensed by Samuel French in your territory. Professional and amateur producers should contact the nearest Samuel French office or licensing partner to verify availability.

CAUTION: Professional and amateur producers are hereby warned that *SONGBOOK* is subject to a licensing fee. Publication of this play(s) does not imply availability for performance. Both amateurs and professionals considering a production are strongly advised to apply to Samuel French before starting rehearsals, advertising, or booking a theatre. A licensing fee must be paid whether the title(s) is presented for charity or gain and whether or not admission is charged. Professional/Stock licensing fees are quoted upon application to Samuel French.

No one shall make any changes in this title(s) for the purpose of production. No part of this book may be reproduced, stored in a retrieval system, or transmitted in any form, by any means, now known or yet to be invented, including mechanical, electronic, photocopying, recording, videotaping, or otherwise, without the prior written permission of the publisher. No one shall upload this title(s), or part of this title(s), to any social media websites.

For all enquiries regarding motion picture, television, and other media rights, please contact Samuel French.

MUSIC USE NOTE

Licensees are solely responsible for obtaining formal written permission from copyright owners to use copyrighted music in the performance of this play and are strongly cautioned to do so. If no such permission is obtained by the licensee, then the licensee must use only original music that the licensee owns and controls. Licensees are solely responsible and liable for all music clearances and shall indemnify the copyright owners of the play(s) and their licensing agent, Samuel French, against any costs, expenses, losses and liabilities arising from the use of music by licensees. Please contact the appropriate music licensing authority in your territory for the rights to any incidental music.

IMPORTANT BILLING AND CREDIT REQUIREMENTS

If you have obtained performance rights to this title, please refer to your licensing agreement for important billing and credit requirements.

INTRODUCTION TO "SONGBOOK"

by The Authors

This is a musical for two females and three males, who play some one hundred parts between them.

It tells of the life and times of the late Moony Shapiro, a songwriter who survived 69 years of whatever the 20th century might throw at him.

SETS & PROPS

As the title suggests, the show should purposely recall the theater anthologies of real-life songwriters — Stephen Sondheim, Noel Coward, Cole Porter, Fats Waller, and others. The style, therefore, can be as economical as a concert performance; or as relatively elaborate as the London and New York productions (directed by Jonathan Lynn) which contained the following elements:

1) An open space with Moony Shapiro memorabilia — his white grand piano, his trunk of trunk songs and souvenirs, his published songs and shows.
2) Drop cloths and simple cut-outs for production numbers from Moony Shapiro's repertoire. (These are listed in the margins of the script by Capital Letters, and a Plot will be found in APPENDIX: 1).
3) Projections depicting places and people from the 1920's to the 1970's to orientate the audience for each incident and musical number, which flow from one to the other in a fluid and fast style. (These are indicated in the script but feel free to add or subtract from this list). Listed in APPENDIX: 3.
4) 2 chairs and a table on each side of the stage, a lampost, an upright piano, a drumkit and a trolley-table with typewriter. These and smaller props are indicated in APPENDIX: 4. This list can be adapted to the scale of your production.
5) In the original production the grand piano, the small upright piano and the drumkit were winched. Cues are listed in the margins of the script by Numbers: Winch plot in APPENDIX: 2. Positions for grand piano indicated: 1st: CENTER STAGE. 2nd: UPSTAGE RIGHT. Drumkit position: CENTER STAGE. Upright position: UPSTAGE LEFT.

The production benefits from being kept simple and inventive. Indeed it can effectively be performed anywhere from a major small theater (with the above values) to concert-style production with the bare minimum. e.g. piano and drapes.

COSTUMES

The COMPANY start dressed as for a typical songwriter anthology—ACTORS in tuxedos, ACTRESSES in dark evening dresses. Other than the production numbers the minimum change is best—hats, shawls, overcoats, jackets, etc.

For the production numbers some over-dressing may be necessary (e.g. dungarees in "Happy Hickory". Busby Berkely skirts for "Pretty Face", various character costumes for "Les Halles" and "East River Rhapsody"). These should be specifically designed for very quick change. The wings are alive with the sound of Velcro.

CHARACTERS

The performers are 3 ACTORS and 2 ACTRESSES who can sing, act, and move. Dancing is an advantage but not essential. Versatility, however, is vital.

ACTOR 1—is the STORYTELLER, an urbane, debonnair, light comedian anchor man. He is in middle-age. He is the only character whose age is specified, owing to the twist at the end of the show. Singing voice: non-legit but good, stylish interpreter of lyrics with an ear for harmony. He also plays Mr. Shapiro, Italian Shoe Shine Boy, Twenties Chorus Boy, Louis Da Rosa, French Crooner, French Street Musician, Bavarian Singer, Vocal Group Singer, British Colonel, Marvin Brennan, Israeli Singer, Russian Singer, Lee-Pyong-Do, Liverpool Group Drummer, "Climber".

ACTOR 2—is MOONY SHAPIRO, a Liverpool Irish orphan with New York Jewish foster parents. A non-heroic figure, fast-moving opportunist with a great belief in himself and the world's goodness despite all he finds to the contrary. Singing voice: non-legit baritone, slightly dissipated by booze and tobacco. Good with lyrics and an ear for harmony. He ages from teenage to old age. He also plays Chinese laundry boy, Bavarian singer, Victory V singer, Senator "Beanpole" Pickles, Villager, "Climber".

ACTRESS 1 – is BELLA SHAPIRO, Moony's wife, a Chicago meat-king's daughter. Vivacious, rebellious, cosmopolitan, strong-willed. Light comedienne. Singing voice: trained mezzo-soprano, good with popular ballads, an ear for harmony with strong top range. She ages from early twenties to old age. She also plays Reverend Mother, Mrs. Shapiro, Mrs. Kleinberg, Twenties Chorus Girl, Torch Singer, Singer With Scarf, Busby Berkely Girl, Bavarian Singer, Vocal Group singer, Marlene Dietrich, Rusty, Israeli Singer, Kim-Sung, Liverpool Group Guitarist, "Climber", Sheila O' Toole.

ACTRESS 2 – is BONNY VAN HEYSEN, Moony's mistress. Bonnie is a well-bred New Yorker who rises from child actress to pop star in the Sixties and Seventies. Nubile, sexy, and funny. Singing voice: trained pop singer, good belter of performance numbers (from Ethel Merman to Edith Piaf). An ear for harmony. She plays parts from age eleven to middle-age. She also plays Tilly, Mae Feldman, Mary Cassidy, Astrid Kalmar, Twenties Chorus Girl, Dolly Ralston, Busby Berkley Girl, French Street Singer, Bavarian Singer, Vocal Group Singer, British Forces Entertainer, Jude, Israeli Singer, Russian Singer, KGB, Lin-Chi, Magda Gyor, Liverpool Group Guitarist.

ACTOR 3 – plays all the other parts. Good-looking young lead actor with gift for impersonation. Guitar-player an advantage. Singing Voice: legit light baritone or tenor with experience and knowledge of many popular styles. An ear for harmony. He plays parts from childhood to middle-age – Dead End Kid, Rabbi Kotchinsky, Sailor, U.S. Immigration Officer, Banjo Player, Newsboy, Rudy Vallee, Bum, Dance Partner, Parisian Man-About-Town, French Waiter, French Flower Seller, Bavarian Singer, Gestapo, Press Photographer, Vocal Group Singer, Newsboy, German Prison Guard, Victory V Singer, Bing Crosby, Dan Dailey, Mario Lanza, Alvin Burns, Chuck, Israeli Singer, Shmuel Levi, Russian Singer, Harold Prince, Johnny Bakuba, Bob Dylan, Bob Dylan Spokesman, Benedict Rickenbacker, Liverpool Group Singer, Trades Union Leader, Clyde.

UNDERSTUDIES (COVERS) – may be used as Pit Singers in the production numbers indicated on the score.

Julian More
Monty Norman
London. 1984

SONGS

ACT ONE

Songbook (from Movie BALTIMORE BALLYHOO)	1948
East River Rhapsody (from Revue FELDMAN FOLLIES OF 1926)	1926
Talking Picture Show (from Movie EVERMORE)	1928
Meg (Trunk Song)	1929
Mister Destiny (Recording)	1930
Your Time is Different from Mine (Recording)	1932
Pretty Face (from Movie PRETTY FACES OF 1934)	1934
Je Vous Aime, Milady (Recording)	1935
Les Halles (Cabaret Song)	1935
Olympics Song (Recording)	1936
Nazi Party Pooper (Trunk Song)	1936
I'm Gonna Take Her Home to Momma (Recording)	1938

WAR SONGS

Bumpity-Bump	1939–45
The Girl In the Window (Das Mädchen Am Fenster)	
Victory V	

HOLLYWOOD EVERGREENS

April In Wisconsin (from Movie A YANK AT THE VATICAN)	1945
It's Only A Show (from Movie LET'S DO THE SHOW RIGHT HERE)	1946
Bring Back Tomorrow (from Movie BRING BACK TOMORROW)	1947
Songbook (Reprise)	1948

ACT TWO

Happy Hickory (Title Song of Musical)   1954

HAPPY HICKORY Rejects (Trunk Songs)

Climbin'
Don't Play That Lovesong Any More

Vocal Gems from HAPPY HICKORY (From the Musical)

Happy Hickory	
Lovely Sunday Mornin'	
Rusty's Dream Ballet	
A Storm In My Heart	
The Pokenhatchit Public Protest Committee	
Happy Hickory (Reprise)	
Happy Hickory (from Tel Aviv and Moscow Productions)	1956
I Accuse (from Musical RED WHITE AND BLACK)	1957
Messages I (Trunk Song)	1958
Messages II (Version for Bob Dylan)	1963
I Found Love (Recording)	1964
Don't Play That Lovesong Any More (Trunk Song)	?
Golden Oldie (Trunk Song)	1972
Climbin' (Recording)	1972
Nostalgia (Trunk Song)	1977
Don't Play That Lovesong Any More (Reprise)	
Songbook (Reprise)	

Songbook

ACT ONE

OVERTURE [MUSIC CUE A]

Projection: SONGBOOK logo.* ACTOR 1 as the STORY-TELLER is alone onstage at the piano. The only other furniture is MOONY SHAPIRO's trunk. Opening [MUSIC CUE 1] [WINCH (PRESET)]

STORYTELLER. (*over music*) Well, here we are again. We've celebrated Cole Porter, Eubie Blake, Noel Coward, Stephen Sondheim, Fats Waller, and Duke Ellington. And tonight, ladies and gentlemen, we celebrate the late, great Moony Shapiro. (*A pause for applause—none!*) Apparently some of you have never heard of Moony Shapiro. *Amazing.* (*Music starts again.*) Okay, if you don't know what made Moony Shapiro a unique songwriter, I'll tell you. His very existence, his life style. Moony moved with the times, traveled the world in search of hit songs. Each experience became a song. Was he not the only songwriter to be snubbed by Adolf Hitler, marry a socialist socialite, escape from Colditz, accompany Margaret Truman, be black-listed by Senator McCarthy, take on the Russian Secret Police, and still find time to write a song or two? Quite a life. Moony Shapiro survived sixty-nine years of whatever the twentieth century might throw at him. And, in so doing, gave us songs to lighten our darkest hour. Ladies and gentlemen, a songwriter, his times, his songs. (*taking a piece of music from the piano*) First the famous Fred Astaire number from "Baltimore Ballyhoo" which I like to think of as Moony Shapiro's theme song—

"SONGBOOK"

STORYTELLER. (*continued*)
HARD TIMES
NEED SOFT WORDS
SWEET RHYMES
AND HUMMING BIRDS . . .
AM I FEELING BLUE?

---

*See page 83.

NOT WHEN I SING
A SONG WITH YOU!

DARK NIGHTS
NEED BRIGHT TUNES.
SOFT LIGHTS
AND HARVEST MOONS . . .
I'M BROKE, SONGS ARE FREE
ROCKEFELLER
WOULD ENVY ME

I'VE GOT A
SONGBOOK IN MY HAND,
AND NOW IT'S ON THE PIANO STAND,
I'LL PLAY A HAPPY SONG FROM MY
SONGBOOK
SONG BOOK . . .

DOWN DAYS
NEED UPBEATS,
ALWAYS
MY HEART REPEATS—
KILL THAT WORRIED LOOK
WITH A SONG FROM YOUR
SONGBOOK.
(*spoken*) And now, ladies and gentlemen, I'd like you to meet my fellow members of The Moony Shapiro Fan Club.

(*The rest of the COMPANY enter.*)

   Actress 1.
HARD TIMES
NEED SOFT WORDS
SWEET RHYMES
AND HUMMING BIRDS . . .
   Actor 3.
AM I FEELING BLUE?
NOT WHEN I SING
A SONG WITH YOU!
   Actress 2.
DARK NIGHTS

NEED BRIGHT TUNES.
SOFT LIGHTS
AND HARVEST MOONS . . .
  Actor 2.
I'M BROKE, SONGS ARE FREE,
ROCKEFELLER
WOULD ENVY ME!

Men.	Women.
I'VE GOT A	OOOOOO . . .
SONGBOOK IN MY HAND,	OOOOOO . . .
AND NOW IT'S ON THE	OOOOOO . . .
PIANO STAND,	
I'LL PLAY A HAPPY	OOOOOO . . .
SONG FROM MY	

  All.
SONGBOOK
SONG BOOK . . .

DOWN DAYS
NEED UPBEATS,
ALWAYS
MY HEART REPEATS—
KILL THAT WORRIED LOOK
WITH A SONG BOOK
WITH A SONG BOOK
WITH A SONG BOOK
SONG BOOK
SONG BOOK
SONG BOOK
(*repeats until CAST drops out*)
  Storyteller. (*indicating piano*) We have here onstage, Moony Shapiro's actual piano.
SONG BOOK
  Actor 3. (*indicating trunk*) Moony Shapiro's very own trunk.
SONG BOOK
(*ACTRESS 2 takes book from top of trunk.*)
  Actress 2. (*holding up book*) Rhyming dictionary.
SONG BOOK
(*ACTRESS 1 takes metronome from top of trunk.*)
  Actress 1. (*holding up metronome*) Metronome.
SONG BOOK
(*ACTOR 2 takes us. Army Officer's Hat from top of trunk.*)

SONGBOOK

Actor 2. Army hat.
SONG BOOK
(*ACTOR 3 takes hip flask from top of trunk.*)
Actor 3. (*holding up hip flask*) Hip flask.
Storyteller. (*producing gold watch*) And a gold watch, given him by his Irish mother. And what did he give us, ladies and gentlemen? Songs. From his trunk . . . (*ACTRESS 2 takes from the trunk a pile of manuscript music tied with a red ribbon and hands it to STORYTELLER.*) . . . trunk songs — songs that express his deepest feelings, very personal, strictly not for publication. (*The music fades.*) We're very grateful to the Shapiro estate for allowing us to sing, for the first time in public, this rare and revealing material. (*STORYTELLER places song pile on stage where it remains for entire show.*) [MUSIC CUE 1A] And, of course, Moony Shapiro evergreens you've whistled and danced to for five decades.

[WINCH CUE: 1]

"APRIL IN WISCONSIN"
[MUSIC CUE 1B]

(*ACTOR 3 takes sheet music from piano, opens it, and sings with ACTRESSES 1 & 2.*)

Actresses 1 & 2, Actor 3.
WHEN IT'S APRIL,
WHEN IT'S APRIL,
WHEN IT'S APRIL IN WISCONSIN,
OOH-OOH,
OOH-OOH . . .
(*All put memorabilia back in trunk.*)
Storyteller. Like this immortal number which I'm sure you all remember . . . (*ACTOR 2 sits at piano as MOONY SHAPIRO.*)
Moony.
WHEN IT'S APRIL IN WISCONSIN
AND I'M SITTING HERE IN ROME,
I AM LONGIN' FOR WISCONSIN
AND MY HUCKLEBERRY HOME . . .

(*The STORYTELLER continues over humming of song —.*)

Storyteller. Little is known of Moony's origins — except this gold watch. Apparently, a well-to-do Liverpool corn merchant's son gave it to an Irish tweeny for services rendered. Moony was the result. (*The music fades. ACTRESSES 1 & 2 and ACTOR 3 exit with trunk. The STORYTELLER hands the watch to MOONY who now wears it. Projection changes to Liverpool Docks.*) Born Michael Mooney, in Liverpool, 1908, he was abandoned by his unfortunate mother, and raised at St Cecilia's Orphanage, [MUSIC CUE 1B] where he played Honky Tonk harmonium when the nuns were out of earshot. (*takes book from piano*) In his autobiography, "Moon in June," he recalls a significant turning point in his early musical education. (*hands book to MOONY*)   [WINCH CUE: 2]

MOONY. (*opens book and reads*) History often repeated itself. I was sixteen and hopelessly in love with Tilly, the orphanage skivvy. One day the Mother Superior caught us together, and dialogue like this you never forget—

(*Enter ACTRESS 1 as REVEREND MOTHER.*)

REVEREND MOTHER. Mother o' God, Michael Mooney, what are you doin' with Tilly?

MOONY. Givin' her a music lesson, Reverend Mother.

REVEREND MOTHER. A *music* lesson?

MOONY. Explainin' the mystery of the missin' black notes between E and F—(*REVEREND MOTHER clouts him.*)—and B and C, Reverend Mother.

REVEREND MOTHER. (*clouting him again*) Then what are Tilly's bloomers doin' hangin' from your harmonium? (*Exit REVEREND MOTHER.*)

MOONY. There was no adequate answer to this, and as the punishment seemed more than usually Jesuitical, I made a dash for the docks, givin' a last prayer that I had not left Tilly in the same condition my mum had been left by my dad—whoever he was. [MUSIC CUE 1C—FIRST START]

(*Enter ACTRESS 2 as TILLY.*)

TILLY. Oh, sweetheart, I'll never see you again!

MOONY. Tilly, take this. (*giving her his gold watch*)—to remember me by.

TILLY. But it was your mum's!

MOONY. It'll bring you luck. (*kisses her*) [MUSIC CUE 1C—SEC-

OND START] (*Exit TILLY. MOONY moves to wings to exchange book for cloth cap and carpet bag.*)

STORYTELLER. Michael Mooney stowed away on the first boat he saw, which happened to be a banana boat bound for Jamaica. [MUSIC CUE 1D] What a trip! Force ten gales, engine trouble, and a tear or two for Tilly. But despite it all, luck was with him. For where did that battered boat reach safe harbor? New York. (*Projection changes to Statue of Liberty.*)

MOONY. New York! A sight beyond my wildest dreams!

STORYTELLER. This was the land of opportunity.

(*Exit STORYTELLER. Enter ACTRESS 1 as MRS. SHAPIRO and ACTOR 3 as DEAD END KID.*)

MRS. SHAPIRO. Help!! (*MRS. SHAPIRO is being attacked by the DEAD END KID who is trying to snatch her handbag. MOONY intervenes. In the fight, MOONY saves MRS. SHAPIRO's handbag. As he is consoling her, the DEAD END KID rips off MOONY's bag and makes a dash for it.*)

MOONY. It was rather more than I had bargained for, half an hour off the boat. All I had were the clothes I stood up in. But all was not lost. For who should that lady turn out to be? None other than Mrs. Shapiro, wife of Abraham Shapiro [MUSIC CUE 1E] the well-known Lower East Side piano teacher.

[WINCH CUE: 3] (*A small upright piano with a menorah on top comes onstage. ACTOR 1 as MR. SHAPIRO sits at it, playing jazz.*)

MR. SHAPIRO. Illegal immigrant, Minnie? That's trouble!
MRS. SHAPIRO. But such a brave boy!
MR. SHAPIRO. Okay. So what? Let him stay a few days.
MOONY. After a few months, those two wonderful people were treating me like their own son. (*MOONY plays a duet with MR. SHAPIRO.*) Including free piano lessons. I was enchanted by Mr. Shapiro's conservatoire of pupils.
MR. SHAPIRO. (*introducing imaginary characters*) My boy, I want you to know George. And his big brother, Ira. And this is Jerome. And Dick. And Larry. And Yip, Irving, Sammy, and Oscar. (*Exit MR. & MRS. SHAPIRO.*)

MOONY. Hi, Oscar. Broadway beckoned. But my name, Michael Mooney, didn't sound right. So, as the Shapiros had virtually adopted me, I adopted their name and decided to become Jewish. I went to see Rabbi Kotschinsky.

(*Enter ACTOR 3 as RABBI.*)

RABBI. You realize, my boy, you'll have to be circumcised.
MOONY. I decided not to become Jewish. Cutting the E from Mooney was less painful, and Shapiro a better name for a songwriter.

(*Enter STORYTELLER with book.*)

STORYTELLER. (*with book*) Ex-chorus girl and impressario's wife, Mae Feldman, recalls in her autobiography, "The Happy Hoofer"—(*exit*)

(*Enter ACTRESS 2 as MAE.*) [WINCH CUE: 4]

MAE. (*like Mae West*) I had a feeling young Moony Shapiro was going to be big. I was not disappointed. He could write songs, too.

"DON'T PLAY THAT LOVESONG ANY MORE"
[MUSIC CUE 1F]

MOONY. (*sings*)
DON'T PLAY THAT LOVESONG ANY MORE, BIX,
YOU BLOW YOUR HORN AND I FEEL BLUE . . .
 MAE. No, no, no! My husband's lookin' for a New York song.
 MOONY. Yes, ma'am.
 MAE. D'ya think ya can come up with it overnight?
 MOONY. Yes, ma'am.
 MAE. Right, boy. Let's play some sheet music. (*Exit MAE.*)
 MOONY. So I wrote a New York song. It was my way of saying, "Thank you, Abe and Minnie Shapiro . . . and thank you, New York."

(*Projection fades.* [MUSIC CUE 2] *A Musical Fanfare. A poster* [FLY CUE: A] *flies in. THE FELDMAN FOLLIES OF 1926 by Rodgers and Hart.*)

MOONY. I was thrilled. And scared. Except for my number, it was a Rodgers and Hart score. I kissed the Shapiro mezuzah and said five Hail Marys. I wasn't taking any chances. (*Exit MOONY.*)

[FLY CUE: B] (*ACTOR 3 enters as SAILOR.*)

"EAST RIVER RHAPSODY"

SAILOR.
THE HOOTING OF A TUGBOAT,
THE HONKING OF A HORN,
THE SWEETEST MUSIC
WAKES ME EVERY MORN.
THE CLANGING OF A TRASH CAN
IN THE EARLY MORNING DAWN—
HOW LOVELY THAT CACOPHONOUS CLASH CAN BE . . .
THAT'S MY EAST RIVER RHAPSODY.

[FLY CUE: C]
[FLY CUE: D]
[FLY CUE: E]
(*Drop in East River Cloth. ACTRESS 1 is MRS. KLEINBERG; ACTRESS 2 is MARY CASSIDY; ACTOR 1 is Italian SHOE SHINE BOY; ACTOR 2 is Chinese LAUNDRY BOY.*)

COMPANY.
EARLY MORNING,
EARLY MORNING . . .
SAILOR.
SHALOM, MRS. KLEINBERG
SO TELL ME, WHAT IS NEW?
   (MRS. KLEINBERG: don't ask!)
TOP O' THE MORNING TO YOU, MARY CASSIDY!
WE GOT A DATE TO EAT AN IRISH STEW!
   (MARY CASSIDY: I'll be at Mick's diner, seven o'clock!)

CAN YOU DO MY LAUNDRY
QUICKLEY, MISTER WU?

MARY WILL BE DRESSED UP
I MUST LOOK GOOD, TOO!

BUON GIORNO, ROCCO BABY,
FOR A DIME-A SHINE-A MY SHOE!
HOW'S YOUR MOMMA? HOW'S YOUR POPPA?
WHAT'S THE WORLD A-DOING TO YOU?
  COMPANY.
NO MUSIC TAKES ME HIGHER
THAN THE MUSIC OF THE LOWER EAST SIDE . . .
  SAILOR.
THE SIREN OF A SQUAD CAR
WHICH COMES AND GOES ALONG,
A DIMLY HEARD SALVATION ARMY SONG,
A BABY WHO'S A SHOUTER,
THE SCHOOLYARD GOING STRONG,
THE WIND WILL TAKE MY MELODY OUT TO SEA . . .
  ALL.
THAT'S MY EAST RIVER
  SAILOR.
EAST RIVER
  ALL.
RHAPSODY

(*During applause two chairs are set.* [MUSIC CUE 2A] *Enter STORYTELLER, taking off SHOE SHINE BOY costume.*) [FLY CUE: F]

STORYTELLER. Moony Shapiro was launched. The first night party, given by young society hostess, Pookie Van Heysen, was packed with Broadway celebrities. Moony was walking on air. He could hardly believe that one song had changed his life. Here were all these people treating him as one of them. Rodgers, Hart, P.G. Wodehouse, Governor Al Smith and a then-unknown actress by the name of Astrid Kalmar, (*The music stops.*) who recalls her first days with Moony in her autobiography, "You're Never Alone with An Ego." [FLY CUE: G]

(*Enter ACTRESS 2 as ASTRID KALMAR.*) [FLY CUE: H]

ASTRID. (*like Greta Garbo*) I don't know whether to curse or bless that party. But you never forget your first true love. I was afraid I would never see him again.

18 SONGBOOK

(*Enter MOONY.*)

MOONY. She was leaving the next day for Hollywood to become a star.

(*Enter ACTOR 3 as U.S. IMMIGRATION with MRS. SHAPIRO.*)

U.S. IMMIGRATION. (*with press clipping*) U.S. Immigration, Mrs. Shapiro. Do you know this man—Michael Mooney?
MRS. SHAPIRO. (*also with press clipping*) Moony Shapiro, you mean. The New York Times picture is better.
U.S. IMMIGRATION. We have reason to believe you have been harboring an illegal immigrant for two years.
MRS. SHAPIRO. Two years? Time flies. [MUSIC CUE 2B] (*Exit U.S. IMMIGRATION and MRS. SHAPIRO.*)
MOONY. The heat was on. And I was off. On the Pullman Express with Astrid. (*Train whistles. MOONY and ASTRID sit on two chairs and bounce up and down with the movement of the train.*)
ASTRID. Four wonderful days! (*Train whistles.*)
MOONY. We never even made it to the diner!
ASTRID. We laughed so much!
MOONY. We loved so much!

[WINCH CUE: 5]   (*Enter STORYTELLER wearing straw boater.*)

STORYTELLER. Cue for song. But in 1926 movies were silent. (*The music stops.*) And nobody wanted a songwriter. [MUSIC CUE 2C]
ASTRID. I went from motion picture to motion picture.
MOONY. I went from movie house to movie house. Playing the piano. What else could I do?
ASTRID. I played with John Barrymore, Buster Keaton, and Ramon Navarro. (*ACTRESS 2 begins onstage change to 20's CHORUS GIRL.*)
MOONY. I'd love to have written songs for them, but who likes silent songs?
STORYTELLER. Then—1927. (*drum roll*) "The Jazz Singer." The talking picture show was born. And Moony wrote his first talking picture song. [MUSIC CUE 3] (*ACTRESSES 1 & 2 as 20's

SONGBOOK 19

CHORUS GIRLS join STORYTELLER. ACTOR 3 plays banjo and sings.)

"TALKING PICTURE SHOW"

LISTEN TO MY FEET DANCE,	For optional 2nd Chorus add — (TAPPING)
LISTEN TO MY VOICE SING,	(YAH-DI-YAH!)
LISTEN TO THE BAND GOIN' VO-DEE-OH	
IN A TALKING PICTURE SHOW	
LISTEN TO MY CLOCK TICK,	(TICKING)
LISTEN TO MY HORSE NEIGH,	(NEIGHING)
LISTEN TO THE SOUND OF THE RODEO	
IN A TALKING PICTURE SHOW.	

THAT MIRACLE OF
 SCIENCE
WE KNOW
IS HERE TO STAY.
THAT POPULAR
 APPLIANCE
SHOWS ME
TALKIN' TO YOU,
I'M HERE TO SAY—

LISTEN TO THE BIG SCENE,	(I LOVE YOU)
LISTEN TO THE KISSES,	(KISSING)
SINGIN' HI-DI-HI AND A-HO-DI-HO	
IN A TALKING PICTURE SHOW.	

LISTEN TO MY FEET　　　(TAPPING)
　DANCE,
LISTEN TO MY VOICE　　(YAH-DI-YAH!)
　SING,
LISTEN TO THE BAND
　GOIN' VO-DEE-OH
IN A TALKING PICTURE
　SHOW

LISTEN TO MY CLOCK　　(TICKING)
　TICK,
LISTEN TO MY HORSE　　(NEIGHING)
　NEIGH,
LISTEN TO THE SOUND
　OF THE RODEO
IN A TALKING PICTURE
　SHOW.

THAT MIRACLE OF
　SCIENCE
WE KNOW
IS HERE TO STAY.
THAT POPULAR
　APPLIANCE
SHOWS ME
TALKIN' TO YOU,
I'M HERE TO SAY—

LISTEN TO THE BIG　　　("I LOVE YA!")
　SCENE,
LISTEN TO THE KISSES,　(KISSING)
SINGIN' HI-DI-HI AND
　A-HO-DI-HO
IN A TALKING PICTURE
　SHOW.
(*dance break*)
LISTEN . . . FEET DANCE,
LISTEN . . . VOICE SING,
LISTEN . . . VO-DEE-OH

IN A TALKING PICTURE
TALKING PICTURE

SONGBOOK

TALKING PICTURE
SHOW . . .
PICTURE SHOW

(*Exit STORYTELLER, ACTRESSES 1 & 2, ACTOR 3 taking off his chair. Projection: Palm Tree. Enter MOONY with large cigar, newspaper and director's chair. He sits.*) [WINCH CUE: 6]

MOONY. So at last I was writing songs in Hollywood. Big deal. In those days a studio songwriter made about as much as a janitor. But I was living like a king in Astrid's Beverly Hills château, imported brick by brick from Bordeaux, France, complete with vineyard. Around this time, Dolly Ralston, Hollywood columnist and all-round-bitch-on-wheels, took her first snide dig at me.

(*Enter ACTRESS 2 as DOLLY RALSTON, with trolley-table with typewriter which she sets in front of chair and sits.*)

STORYTELLER. (*reads paper*) Major star weds Minor Musician. Can the duet last? So far Moony and Astrid are very amicable about money. Astrid pays the bills and Moony leaves the tips.
DOLLY RALSTON. (*like Hedda Hopper, typing*) A little songbird tells me of ruffled feathers in a certain Beverly Hills love nest. Could it be hubby's ever-growing shopping list?

(*ACTRESS 2 begins fast onstage change to ASTRID.*)

MOONY. A Rolls Royce for Astrid. A Ming dynasty vase for Bugsy who got me my U.S. citizenship. A Cartier tiepin for me. A pair of Bechsteins for me. A polo pony for guess who? Me.

(*ACTRESS 2 is now ASTRID again.*)

ASTRID. With my money!
MOONY. I started to play the stockmarket.
ASTRID. With my money!
MOONY. My stockbroker pal, Maxwell Chesterfield, had gotten me in on some pretty hot investments.
ASTRID. With my money! (*Exit ASTRID with table and chair.*)
MOONY. I felt like Midas. Everything I touched turned to blue

chips. Abe and Minnie Shapiro were visiting with us. I got them in on the bonanza, too.

(*Enter MR. & MRS. SHAPIRO with suitcase.*)

MR. SHAPIRO. What's to lose, Minnie? After all, the money's only sitting in the bank.
MRS. SHAPIRO. If Moony says it's alright, then it's alright.
MOONY. It was all wrong. Two weeks later the Shapiros had lost everything. [MUSIC CUE 3A] (*MR. & MRS. SHAPIRO crumple and exit sadly. Enter ASTRID.*)
ASTRID. My money! (*music out*) Get out. (*ACTRESS 2 begins fast onstage change to DOLLY.*)
MOONY. I felt like emptying the pool, and diving from the top board. As for Maxie, he dived—right off the top of the Empire State Building.

(*ACTOR 3 crosses over as NEWSBOY, taking off director's chair.*)

NEWSBOY. Read all about it! Maxwell Chesterfield suicide!

(*ACTRESS 2 is now DOLLY again.*)

DOLLY. Isn't the Wall Street Crash becoming a bore? I'm tired of reporting suicides. Now for the good news. Moony Shapiro has left Hollywood. (*Projection changes to Times Square.*)
MOONY. I went back to New York to see the man in my life, music publisher Louis da Rosa, who described me in his autobiography, "Tin Pan Alleycats."

[WINCH CUE: 7] (*Enter ACTOR 1 as LOUIS DA ROSA, smoking cigar.*)

DA ROSA. Moony drank a helluva lot of black coffee that morning in my 28th Street office. He stank of bathtub gin. He had been fired by the studio. I asked him—(*to MOONY*) What about you and Astrid?
MOONY. Give me a drink and I'll tell you!
DA ROSA. By his face, he didn't have to tell me. So I didn't have to give him a drink. I told him—forget your troubles, write a song for the crooner, Rudy Vallee.
MOONY. *The* Rudy Vallee?

DA ROSA. Sure. He's one of my dearest friends.
MOONY. Boy, have I got a song for you! This is the greatest song I've ever written. I'll never be able to write another one like it. Listen—

"DON'T PLAY THAT LOVESONG ANY MORE"
[MUSIC CUE 3B]

MOONY.
DON'T SING THAT LOVESONG ANY MORE, RUDY,
YOU CROON AND ALL THE GIRLS GO WILD . . .
  DA ROSA. I hate it.
  MOONY. You're right. How about this—?
  DA ROSA. Ten o'clock, Thursday.
  MOONY. Right!
  DA ROSA. I called in Rudy Vallee.

(*Enter ACTOR 3 as RUDY VALLEE with megaphone.*)

"MELODY OF WHIFFENPOOF SONG"
[MUSIC CUE 3C]

RUDY. (*through megaphone, croons—*)
I'M LOOKING FOR A LOVESONG AT THE PLACE
WHERE LOUIS DWELLS . . .
  DA ROSA. H'ya, Rudy.
  RUDY. H'ya, Louis.
  DA ROSA. Good to see you. Better to hear you. Let me take your megaphone. Have I got a lovesong for you!
  RUDY. That's what I'm here for.
  DA ROSA. Bing wants it. But you've got it.
  RUDY. Bing who?
  DA ROSA. Listen to this! The boy's a genius.

(*MOONY takes a swig from his hip flask, takes music from trunk song pile and sits at piano.*)

"MEG"
[MUSIC CUE 4]

MOONY. (*sings drunkenly*)
I LOVE MEG O'FLANAGAN
MEG O'FLYNN

AND MEG O'DONOVAN TOO
I LOVE MEG O'HARA AND MEG O'NEIL
BUT THE BEST OF THE MEGS IS YOU

MEG O'PHONE
YOU'RE THE SWEETEST THING I'VE EVER KNOWN
I GET TINGLES IN MY FINGERTIPS
WHEN I PRESS YOU TO MY LIPS

MEG O'PHONE
THROUGH YOUR APERTURE I SOFTLY MOAN
I CARESS YOU LIKE YOU WERE MY WIFE
I'D GIVE AN ARM AND LEG
MY LITTLE GOLDEN MEG
IF ONLY YOU WOULD COME TO LIFE

(*MOONY collapses and passes out. Furious, RUDY gets up. DA ROSA hands him his megaphone.*)

RUDY. Thanks a lot! (*RUDY storms out. DA ROSA picks MOONY up and gives him a rough time.*)

DA ROSA. What kind of crap is that for a Rudy Vallee love song? Put it back in your trunk and forget it. I kicked him out, all the way down. But he had a lot further to go down yet. Moony found himself in the Tombs prison — among petty thieves, alcoholics, drug addicts, male prostitutes, pimps.

MOONY. It was like Hollywood — without the swimming pools. [MUSIC CUE 4A]

(*Enter ACTOR 3 as BUM.*)

BUM. (*Harvard accent*) Could you let me have a cigarette? (*pause*) Don't you recognize me? (*pause*) I used to be president of your bank.

MOONY. (*handing him cigarette*) I gave him my last cigarette. And he gave me a bit of advice. All experience is rich. If you use
[WINCH CUE: 8] it right, it can make you richer. (*Music out, exit BUM. Projection changes to Statue of Liberty in black & white.*)

DA ROSA. Moony was growing up. And the outcome was one of the most popular songs of the Depression.

(*Enter ACTRESS 1 as TORCH SINGER.*)

SONGBOOK

"MISTER DESTINY" [MUSIC CUE 5]

TORCH SINGER.
NOT A DIME IN THE BANK,
EV'RY CHECK IS A BLANK,
AND MY MAN SINGS AN OUT-OF-WORK SONG.
WHEN HE LINES UP FOR SOUP
WITH THE REST OF THE GROUP,
MISTER DESTINY, YOU DONE HIM WRONG!

THOUGH HE HELPED WIN THE WAR,
WHAT THE HECK WAS IT FOR?
UNCLE SAM CLEAN FORGOT HIM AND ME.
WHY OH WHY IS OUR FATE
JUST A BIG EMPTY PLATE?
I'M TALKIN' TO YA, MISTER D!

HE'S ONLY A BEGGAR,
NOT A BOOT-LEGGER,
AND OUR HOME AIN'T SUPER-DE-LUXE,
LIVIN' ON THE FREIGHT TRAINS,
WAITIN' FOR THE LATE TRAINS,
THROWN IN JAIL JUST FOR STEALIN' TWO BUCKS.
IS THIS A LAND FIT FOR HEROES?

(*Music continues. Exit TORCH SINGER.*)

DA ROSA. (*moved to tears*) What a song! I always knew the kid would land headfirst on his feet again. Radio and recording stars fell over themselves to sing his songs. All except one, that is. Pity about Rudy Vallee.

(*Enter ACTRESS 2 as DOLLY.*) [WINCH CUE: 9]

DOLLY. Rumor hath it, Moony Shapiro is hoping for a reprise of his duet with Astrid Kalmar. Can they ever be in tune again?

(*ACTRESS 2 begins fast onstage change to ASTRID. Projection changes to New York Skyline at Night.*)

MOONY. I wanted her to see the swell Park Avenue penthouse I had rented. I invited her to spend Christmas amid the wall-to-wall Picassos.

(*ACTRESS 2 is ASTRID again.*)

ASTRID. New York in winter?
MOONY. I sent her two dozen roses every day.
ASTRID. He forgot. Roses make me sneeze.
MOONY. I wrote her poems.
ASTRID. I always hated his lyrics.
MOONY. I kept phoning her.
ASTRID. Always five a.m., my time.
MOONY. That late?
ASTRID. He never owned a watch.
MOONY. I left messages.
ASTRID. They weren't answered.
MOONY. And finally I got the message. It made a quite a song.

[WINCH CUE: 10] (*Exit MOONY and ASTRID, opposite sides of stage.*)

"YOUR TIME IS DIFFERENT FROM MINE" [MUSIC CUE 6]

(*Enter ACTRESS 1 as SINGER WITH SCARF. The scarf is very long and used to comic effect.*)

SINGER WITH SCARF.
THE TELEPHONE DOESN'T RING,
I'M WAITIN' HERE ON A STRING.
OUTSIDE THE AUTUMN LEAVES FALL
AND I SUDDENLY RECALL
YOUR TIME IS DIFFERENT FROM MINE.

THE OTHER SIDE OF THE GLOBE,
YOU WEAR YOUR TANGERINE ROBE,
YOU'RE IN A TROPICAL NIGHT,
FIREFLIES ARE BURNING BRIGHT.
YOUR TIME IS DIFFERENT FROM MINE.

DARLIN', I KEEP ON REHEARSIN'
ALL THAT I'LL SAY TO YOU WHEN
I HEAR THAT PERSON-TO-PERSON
REVERSIN' THE CHARGES AGAIN . . .

CAN ONLY GUESS WHAT GOES ON,
OR WHERE YOU ARE NOW YOU'VE GONE.
WHY'S THERE NO SOUND FROM MY PHONE?

MAYBE YOU ARE NOT ALONE!
YOUR TIME IS DIFFERENT FROM MINE.

(*Enter ACTOR 3 as DANCE PARTNER. He joins SINGER WITH SCARF in a comic pas-de-deux of melodramatic passion. Exit DANCE PARTNER.*) [WINCH CUE: 11]

SINGER WITH SCARF. (*continued*)
CAN ONLY GUESS WHAT GOES ON,
OR WHERE YOU ARE NOW YOU'VE GONE.
WHY'S THERE NO SOUND FROM MY PHONE?
MAYBE YOU ARE NOT ALONE!
YOUR TIME IS DIFFERENT FROM MINE.

(*Exit SINGER WITH SCARF. Enter DOLLY RALSTON.*)

DOLLY. October 14, 1933. Boo hoo. Your columnist used a dozen handkerchiefs over the forthcoming divorce of fading film star, Astrid Kalmar, and hit songwriter, Moony Shapiro. He is citing Nelson, Clark, Franchot, Gary, and the Barrymores — Lionel, John and Ethel.

(*Exit DOLLY. Projection changes to Eiffel Tower. Enter MOONY.*)

MOONY. In the old Yiddish phrase, "Spielkus in tokis," I had pins and needles in my backside. I just couldn't sit still — even in success. Armed with introductions to Henry Miller, Hemingway, and all the intellectuals, I went to Paris, France. I learned French. I needn't have bothered. [MUSIC CUE 7] Paris seemed to be fifty million Americans, burning the candle at all ends. I had visions of twice nightly orgies — (*sings*)
OH THOSE NIGHTS OF BEAUJOLAIS AND BUTTOCKS!

(*Exit MOONY. Enter STORYTELLER.*)

STORYTELLER. A bit strong for Hollywood in those days. But the line leads to one of the first Americans-in-Paris songs. Moony sent it home to Busby Berkely for his motion picture, "Pretty Faces of 1934."

(*Exit STORYTELLER. Enter ACTOR 3 as PARISIAN MAN-ABOUT-TOWN.*)

"PRETTY FACE"

Parisian Man-About-Town.
OH THOSE NIGHTS OF BEAUJOLAIS AND BAWDY,
WOOING ALL LES GIRLS OF MONTPARNASSE.
OH THOSE NIGHTS SO GLAMOROUS AND GAUDY,
ACTING OUT MY ONE-MAN FEYDEAU FARCE—
WITH MANNEQUINS FROM MOLYNEUX
TO WINE AND DINE,
A PRETTY LITTLE POETESS
CHEZ GERTRUDE STEIN,
A FEW WHITE RUSSIAN PRINCESSES,
IN FACT, ALL SORTS—
LIKE THOSE CULTURAL CAMP-FOLLOWERS
MARYLOU AND SADIE SCHWARTZ . . .

(*Exit PARISIAN MAN-ABOUT-TOWN. Enter ACTRESSES 1 & 2 as BUSBY BERKELY GIRLS. GIRLS sing and dance a la Dolly Sisters.*)

Girls.
I'M NOT JUST A PRETTY FACE
WHICH IS WHAT YOU MIGHT SUSPECT.
UNDERNEATH YOU'RE GONNA FIND THAT I'VE GOT INTELLECT.

I'M NOT JUST A DIZZY BLONDE.
ALL THE COLLEGE GUYS I'VE PAL-ED
KNOW THAT I HAVE READ THE WORKS OF F. SCOTT FITZGER-ALD.
NO, I'M NO FLOOZIE.
GEE, I'M CHOOSEY!
MY NEW FELLOW
STRUMS A CELLO.
MEASURE MY BROW.
AIN'T IT HIGHBROW?
READIN' SCHOPENHAUER
HOUR AFTER HOUR.
THERE IS MORE TO ME THAN MEETS THE NAKED
  EYE . . .

I'M NOT JUST A COMELY SHAPE.
I GOT INTELLECTUAL PACE.
PLEASE REMEMBER I'VE A BRAIN, FORGET MY
PRETTY FACE!

SCIENTIFICALLY.
YOU'RE TERRIFICALLY
ALL MINE.
EINSTEIN. BRRR . . .

I'M NOT JUST A DUMMY DUMB,
WHAT A LOVELY VOICE I'VE GOT
WHEN I'M READIN' POETRY BY T.S.
ELI-OT.
I'M NOT JUST A VAPID VAMP,
IF I EVER WAS SEDOOCED.
WHO'S THE GUY I'D LOVE TO HAVE? WELL, I GUESS
MARCEL PROUST.
OH, SHOSTAKOVITCH
KNOWS I KNOW VITCH
TOONS ARE HIS TOONS,
NOT SHOW BIZ TOONS.
I CAN GAZE AT,
DAYS AND DAYS AT
MY SURREALISTIC
HIGHLY MODERNISTIC
PICTURE OF THE MONA LISA WITH MUSTACHE . . .
I'M NOT JUST A BROAD ABROAD.
I'M THE TOAST OF LA COUPOLE.
WITH A NICE BOHEMIAN BEAU, I AIN'T NO
PRETTY DOLL
ROUND THE PLACE.
BELIEVE ME
I'M NO HEAD CASE
I'VE GOT AN INTELLECT
TREAT IT WITH DUE RESPECT
OR KISS MY
PRETTY FACE.

(*BLACKOUT. Projection, Gare de Lyon. Enter MOONY with two chairs.*)

MOONY. I had to get out of town fast, anywhere, just for a week's sleep. But I never got further than the Gare de Lyon.

(*Enter STORYTELLER with table.*)

STORYTELLER. For it was at this romantic railroad station that he bumped into the woman who was to play such an important role in his life.

(*He stays and watches scene. Enter ACTRESS 1 as BELLA with fur coat slung over shoulders. MOONY and she collide.*)

BELLA. (*holding her arm, yelling*) Ouch!
MOONY. Sorry.

(*MOONY helps her to a table. They sit. ACTOR 3 as FRENCH WAITER brings two brandies and exits.*)

BELLA. Clumsy sonofabitch. I think I'm going to faint.
STORYTELLER. Moony bought her a brandy. She was wearing white mink which blended beautifully with her sling. (*BELLA reveals her arm in a sling.*)
MOONY. What happened to your arm?
BELLA. Bullet wound.
MOONY. How?
BELLA. Asturias.
MOONY. What's that?
BELLA. Asturias, Spain! Haven't you heard of the Spanish Miners Revolution? The country's in chaos. There could be Civil War — and you don't even know the place exists!

(*Projection fades. Enter DOLLY RALSTON.*)

DOLLY. Is it red roses for a Red Lady? Socialist socialite, Lady Arabella Klintoch, estranged wife of the Earl of Klintoch and disinherited daughter of Chicago meat king, Paxton Rickenbacker, is hitting the night spots with footloose commoner, Moony Shapiro. My Parisian spies tell me they are head over heels in love. (*Exit DOLLY. Projection Moulin Rouge.*)
BELLA. I love you, Moony!
MOONY. Je vous aime, Milady! [MUSIC CUE 8]
BELLA. Sounds like a song title.
MOONY. (*taking out pencil and scribbling*) Hey, not bad! But . . . something more romantic than a station meeting.

BELLA. How about . . . the Orient Express?
MOONY. Change station buffet to Wagons-Lit!
BELLA. For Jean Sablon!
MOONY. With Django Rheinhardt on guitar!

(*ACTOR 1 takes large black fedora from wings, leans against the proscenium and becomes FRENCH CROONER. Comic business trying to get cigarette to light throughout song.*)

"JE VOUS AIME, MILADY"

FRENCH CROONER. (*like Jean Sablon*)
JE VOUS AIM-E
MILADY,
JE VOUS AIM-E,
ET JE SUIS
DANS LE MEME
WAGON-LIT.
LA COINCIDENCE EST EXTRAORDINAIRE-E
QUE JE RENCONTR-E CETTE JOLIE ETRANGER-E
JE VOUS AIM-E,
MILADY,
JE VOUS AIM-E.
VOUS ETES VRAI-
MENT LA CREME
DE LA CREM-E.
ET POUR
QUELQUES JOURS
NOUS AURONS LA MEME ADRESSE:
WAGON TROIS, L'ORIENT EXPRESS.
JE VOUS AIM-E,
MILADY,
JE VOUS AIM-E.

(*On last note FRENCH CROONER finally gets his cigarette alight and coughs. Exit FRENCH CROONER. Drop in cloth of Les Halles Market. Enter ACTRESS 2 as FRENCH STREET SINGER.*) [FLY CUE: 1]

"LES HALLES" [MUSIC CUE 9]

FRENCH STREET SINGER.
THERE'S A MARKET,
AFTER DARK IT

COMES ALIVE,
WHEN THE FRUIT AND THE FLOWERS
ALL ARRIVE.
WHEN THE MEAT SHOPS
AND THE FISH SHOPS
MAKE A SHOW,
IN THE WEE SMALL HOURS,
LET'S GO!

IF WE'RE GONNA MAKE A NIGHT OF IT,
LAST STOP
LES HALLES!
YOU'LL ADORE THE VERY SIGHT OF IT,
TIP TOP
LES HALLES!

YOU'LL SEE A PORTER
WITH MEAT ON HIS BACK,
A MILLIONAIRE'S DAUGHTER
IN A BIG WHITE CADILLAC.
PEOPLE IN GREAT VARIETY
MEET AT LES HALLES!
TOP AN' BOTTOM OF SOCIETY
LOVE THAT LES HALLES!
DRINK ONION SOUP
WITH YOUR HAND ON MY KNEE
IN LES HALLES
WITH A GAL
LIKE ME.

(*MOONY and BELLA get up from their table. He buys her a flower from ACTOR 3 as FLOWER SELLER. A STREET MUSICIAN plays a cornet, while MOONY and BELLA dance a Java.*)

THERE'S A MARKET
AFTER DARK IT
ALWAYS HUMS,
AND YOU PRAY THAT THE DAYLIGHT
NEVER COMES,
WHERE THE LOVERS,

AND THE LOAFERS
LIKE TO STAY
TILL THE BAD, SAD GREY LIGHT
OF DAY.

IF WE'RE DRINKING FOR THE HELL OF IT
LET'S TOAST
LES HALLES!
YOU'LL ADORE THE VERY SMELL OF IT,
YOUR HOST
LES HALLES!
YOU'LL SEE THAT PORTER
SO GLAD THAT HE MET
THE MILLIONAIRE'S DAUGHTER
WITH HER GAULOISE CIGARETTE . . .
(*ALL exit, except FRENCH STREET SINGER. They take table and chairs.*)
AH! AH! LES HALLES!
LOVE AFFAIRS ARE ALWAYS
WILDER IN HIGH CLASS . . . LES HALLES!

YOU'LL DRINK CHAMPAGNE
FROM MY SAWDUSTY SHOE
IN LES HALLES
I'M THE GAL
FOR YOU.

(*Exit FRENCH STREET SINGER. Cloth flies out revealing rest of COMPANY in Bavarian Costume. Projection: Olympics Insignia. They do a thigh-slapping and foot stamping dance, joined by ACTRESS 2.*) [FLY CUE: J]

"OLYMPICS SONG" [MUSIC CUE 10]

COMPANY.
THE PEOPLE ARE MAKING THEIR WAY TO BERLIN,
TO BERLIN TO JOIN THE OLYMPIC GAMES.
UNITED THAT WONDERFUL LEAGUE OF NATIONS.
COMPETITION
IS THE ONLY KIND OF AMMUNITION.
SPORTSMEN ARE COMING INTO THE LIMELIGHT.

IN BERLIN, THEY ALL HOPE TO MAKE THEIR NAMES.
THE RACES ARE FULL OF A GRAND GEMUTLICHKEIT
AT THE THIRTY-SIX OLYMPIC GAMES.

(Exit ALL except ACTOR 1 who throws his Bavarian gear into wings, takes book and is STORYTELLER again.)

STORYTELLER. That was Moony's hit contribution to the jolly festivities of international sport. As a result, he and Bella were among the thousand guests invited to the Olympics party by Doctor Josef Goebbels, who recalls in his Diaries—*(reading from book in thick German accent)* "Party a great success. Only one unfortunate incident concerning the black American athlete, Jesse Owens, and a white American songwriter, whose name escapes me."

(Exit STORYTELLER with exaggerated Goebbels limp. Enter MOONY and BELLA.)

MOONY. What's wrong? Have I got leprosy or something? Why wouldn't Hitler shake my hand?
BELLA. Shapiro is a Jewish name.
MOONY. Well, he snubbed my friend Jesse Owens, too. And Owens is a Welsh name.
BELLA. Jesse's black, Moony. And not from Welsh coal dust. Don't you know about anything but songs? *(Exit BELLA. Projection fades.)*
MOONY. There was worse to come. Next day Bella was late for lunch. Our bags were packed. We had a train to catch. I couldn't think where she was. She said she'd only be an hour visiting an old friend. I waited and waited. At ten after three, I got a call. From the Gestapo.

(Enter ACTOR 3 as GESTAPO.)

GESTAPO. We have some questions to ask you, Herr Shapiro.
MOONY. Likewise. Where's Lady Klintoch?
GESTAPO. In the next room. What is your connection with Dana Hoffman?
MOONY. Never heard of him.
GESTAPO. Her.
MOONY. Her.

GESTAPO. Come now, Herr Shapiro, your "friend" visited the house this morning. Frau Hoffman is a well-known anti-Nazi.

MOONY. Look, can I call my Embassy, please?

GESTAPO. What was your "friend" doing in Asturias, Spain in 1934? (*silence*) Did you know she helped the Union de Hermanos Proletarios? (*silence*) You are Jewish, Herr Shapiro, are you not?

MOONY. Good question. I was about to ask you the same thing.

GESTAPO. Of course, I am a pure-bred Aryan.

MOONY. Pure-bred? You mean, like a poodle? Ever been to a dog show, Buddy? Seen those poor poodles twitching and shivering? That's pure-bred for you. Whereas the mongrels like me—a touch of Irish, sort of Jewish, maybe a little bit of Black somewhere—we mongrels don't give a damn for anyone—including you poodles.

GESTAPO. It is lucky the Fuehrer likes your song, Herr Shapiro.

(*Enter BELLA in a state of shock. MOONY comforts her.*)

MOONY. Darling, are you okay? (*She nods, he turns to "GESTAPO."*) I'm gonna write your Fuehrer another song! One that he won't like nearly so much!

(*Exit MOONY and GESTAPO. Projection: Plaza Hotel, New York. Enter DOLLY RALSTON with radio mike.*)

DOLLY. Hi, there! Here's Dolly Ralston in New York giving you last night's lowdown on high life. Well, Moony Shapiro's done it again. At Pookie Van Heysen's party at the Plaza's Persian Room, Moony rocked the Social Register by singing a song in very bad taste. (*exit*)

(*Enter MOONY. He picks up song from trunk song pile. Fanfare* [MUSIC CUE 10A] *sits at white piano, on which stands a large candelabra.*) [WINCH CUE: 12]

"*NAZI PARTY POOPER*" [MUSIC CUE 11]

MOONY.
SEATED ONE DAY AT THE REICHSTAG
YOUR FUEHRER IST MOODY UND MEAN.

MEIN BEAUTIFUL BERLIN OLYMPICS
VOSS TO SHOW OFF MY NAZI MACHINE.
SO JESSE OWENS
JESSE OWENS
VHY DID YOU SPOIL MY WAGNERIAN SCENE?
(*Projection changes to Jesse Owens at the start of a race.*)
I PUT OUT ZE BANNERS,
I ORDERED GOOD MANNERS,
UND SCHMILING GESTAPO
ALL OVER ZE PLACE.

ZEN ZE STARTER
PULLS ZE TRIGGER
AND ZAT ANIMAL,
ZAT NIGGER
HAS TO GO AND VIN ZE HUNDRED METER RACE!

ZE HOTEL KEMPINSKI'S
AS FRIENDLY AS MINSKY'S
TO EV'RY DELIGHTFUL
AMERICAN JEW,
TILL ZE PAPERS
ALL ARE PLASTERED
WIZ ZE HEADLINES
ZAT ZE BASTARD
VINS ZAT DAMNABLE TWO-HUNDRED METERS, TOO!

YOU'RE A NAZI PARTY POOPER, JESSE OWENS,
AND MY NAZI PARTY SINKS YOU OUGHTA GO,
AND ONE DAY VE VILL SEDDLE
YOU FOR TAKING EV'RY MEDAL.
YOU'RE A NAZI PARTY POOPER, JESSE O.

I VISH IT WAS RAINY
SO DEAR LITTLE LENI
WOULD NOT GET HER MOVIE
OF MY LIVING HELL.

ALL MY TROUBLE
VOS BEGINNING
VEN ZIS SCHWARZER
STARTED VINNING—

GOTT IN HIMMEL, NOW ZE BROAD JUMP'S HIS AS VELL.

WHY AIN'T HE BAVARIAN,
ZIS BLACKFACE BARBARIAN?
A RACE ZAT IS MASTER
SHOULD VIN EV'RY GAME.
VEN ZIS NATIVE
RECORD BEATER
VINS ZE DAMN FOUR
HUNDRED METER
RELAY, I COULD PISS IN ZAT OLYMPIC FLAME!

YOU'RE A NAZI PARTY POOPER, JESSE OWENS,
AND MY NAZI PARTY SINKS YOU OUGHTA GO,
AND ONE DAY VE VILL SEDDLE
YOU FOR TAKING EV'RY MEDAL.
YOU'RE A NAZI PARTY POOPER,
SUPERMAN, YOU'RE NOT SO SUPER!
YOU'RE A NAZI PARTY POOPER, JESSE O.

(*Projection fades. Enter DOLLY, again with radio mike.*) [WINCH CUE: 13]

DOLLY. I would like to assure Herr Hitler that not all Americans are so foul-mouthed and unfair. You're doing a grand job, Adolf. (*Exit DOLLY.*)

MOONY. I hoped Minnie and Abe Shapiro would get a big kick out of the publicity for my anti-Hitler song. But they refused to see me. This was a double blow. Not only did I want them to meet Bella, but I was now in a position to make right the heavy financial loss they had suffered in 1929. So I called in on them, unexpected.

(*Enter MR. AND MRS. SHAPIRO.*)

MR. SHAPIRO. Thank you very much, Moony.
MRS. SHAPIRO. Very thoughtful of you.
MR. SHAPIRO. We wouldn't take a dime. You see, my boy, it's like this—(*He hesitates.*) Minnie, you—
MRS. SHAPIRO. What Abe is trying to say, Moony, is—we've loved you like a son. We've kept all your press cuttings. But this with Germany. How could you go to such an anti-semitic place?

MOONY. I didn't realize.
MRS. SHAPIRO. You write songs for Hitler.
MOONY. For the Olympic Games.
MRS. SHAPIRO. You meet Hitler.
MOONY. I didn't. He turned his back on me.
MRS. SHAPIRO. The New York Times is a liar? (*Exit MR. AND MRS. SHAPIRO.*)
MOONY. It was an understandable misunderstanding. I had been getting some pretty confusing publicity. As so often happened, Bella came to my rescue.

(*Enter BELLA.*)

BELLA. Darling, there's a Nazi rally in Central Park, so naturally I'll be at the anti-Nazi demonstration.

(*Projection: Central Park, New York*)

MOONY. That demonstration of Bella's gave me a golden opportunity to show Abe and Minnie Shapiro exactly where I stood. I hired the best publicity agent in town for maximum press coverage.

(*MOONY and BELLA hold hands and sing.*)

"*THE INTERNATIONALE*" [MUSIC CUE 11A]

BELLA & MOONY.
SO, COMRADES, COME RALLY
AND THE LAST FIGHT LET US FACE,
THE INTERNATIONAL-E
UNITES THE HUMAN RACE

(*ACTOR 3 as PRESS PHOTOGRAPHER crosses over and takes a flash photo of them. Enter DOLLY.*)

DOLLY. Which socialist socialite with what pinko tunesmith sang the Internationale in Central Park? No prizes for guessing, folks. See photograph. (*Exit, projection fades.*)
MOONY. My press coverage filled many pages of Minnie Shapiro's scrapbook. Abe and she were happy. I was the good son again. And to make them even happier, Bella's divorce came

through. The Liverpool Irish Catholic and the Chicago Protestant had a Jewish wedding reception. [MUSIC CUE 12] I promoted Lady Arabella Klintoch to Mrs. Moony Shapiro, and it inspired one of the biggest hits of 1938. (*Exit MOONY.*)

(*Projection: Big Band. ACTRESS 1 joins ACTRESS 2, ACTORS 1 & 3 who enter and form VOCAL GROUP around radio mike.*)

"I'M GONNA TAKE HER HOME TO MOMMA"

I'M GONNA TAKE HER HOME TO MOMMA
'COS AT LAST SHE WILL SAY "YES"
I'M GONNA TAKE HER HOME TO MOMMA
WHO'S GONNA CHOOSE HER WEDDING DRESS.
SHE'LL ORGANIZE A TEN-TIER WEDDING CAKE
AND A WELL-SPRUNG BRIDAL BED.
I'M GONNA TAKE HER HOME TO MOMMA
AND POPPA,
AND THEN I WILL BE WED.

I'M GONNA TAKE HER HOME TO MOMMA
'COS AT LAST SHE WILL SAY "YES"
OH YES
I'M GONNA TAKE HER HOME TO MOMMA
WHO'S GONNA CHOOSE HER WEDDING DRESS.
SHE'LL ORGANIZE A TEN-TIER WEDDING CAKE
AND A WELL-SPRUNG BRIDAL BED.
DOO WAH, DOO WAH, DOO WAH DOO
I'M GONNA TAKE HER HOME TO MOMMA
AND POPPA,

AND SISTERS, BECKY, RACHEL, AND MOLLY,
BROTHERS DANIEL, JACOB, AND SOLLY,
COUSINS BERNIE, MOTTLE, AND IZZY,
RUBIE, SHIRLEY, ESTHER, AND LIZZIE,
AUTIES EDNA, RUTHIE, AND FRANNY,
UNCLES MARTY, MILTON, AND MANNY,
AND MY CALIFORNIAN UNCLE,
WEALTHY UNCLE ED.
THEN I WILL BE WED.

(BLACKOUT)

(*Enter STORYTELLER.*)

STORYTELLER. September 3rd, 1939.

(*Enter ACTOR 3 as NEWSBOY with papers.*)

NEWSBOY. Stop press. Hollywood columnist, Dolly Ralston, run over on Sunset Strip. (*Exit NEWSBOY.*)
STORYTELLER. Of course, that wasn't the only momentous event of the day. A war was declared in Europe.

(*Enter MOONY and BELLA.*)

BELLA. What are you going to do, Moony?
MOONY. Well, I'm not going to the funeral.
BELLA. I mean — what are you going to do? About the war?
STORYTELLER. Moony was surprised to find he was a patriot. Roots are roots — even for a Liverpool Irish orphan with American citizenship and a Jewish surname.
MOONY. Okay, I'll join up. So long, Louis.

(*ACTOR 1 puts cigar in mouth and becomes DA ROSA again.*)

DA ROSA. Where are you going?
MOONY. To join up.
DA ROSA. You mean, you're deserting me?
MOONY. I'm gonna fight for one of my countries.
DA ROSA. Who's gonna write my songs?
MOONY. Don't worry, I've got a new song for you.

"DON'T PLAY THAT LOVESONG ANY MORE"
[MUSIC CUE 12A]

DON'T CROON THAT LOVESONG ANY MORE, BING,
I'M BLUE WHEN YOU SING B-B-BOO . . .
DA ROSA. On second thoughts, desert me. Take care, soldier.
[MUSIC CUE 12B]
MOONY. Thanks, Louis.
BELLA. 'Bye, Moony.
MOONY. So long, Bella.
BELLA. Keep smiling.
MOONY. Chin up. (*They kiss. Exit BELLA, waving. He waves back. Projection: Big Ben, London.*) So once again I made a

dash for the docks. I took the first boat to England. I contacted my old friend, Colonel James Roosevelt and told him, "Jimmy, I wanna join your American Volunteer Force." He politely declined, but gave me a letter to Winston Churchill, who gave me a letter to Lord Mountbatten, who gave me a letter to Noel Coward, who gave me a pencil and said, "Dear boy, write us some morale-boosting war songs." Well, we can't all be heroes.

(*Enter ACTRESS 2 as BRITISH FORCES ENTERTAINER, in RAF male uniform.*)

"BUMPITY-BUMP" [MUSIC CUE 13]

ENTERTAINER.
I MET HER
WITH A BUMPITY-BUMP
WITH A BUMPITY-BUMP
IN THE BLACKOUT
MY HEART WENT
WITH A BUMPITY-BUMP
WITH A BUMPITY-BUMP
IN THE BLACKOUT.
I PUT OUT MY LEFT HAND,
I PUT OUT MY RIGHT.
I FELT HER BUMPITY-BUMP
IN THE BLACKED OUT NIGHT.
I TURNED IN A CIRCLE,
I STUCK OUT MY FACE,
AND KISSED HER BUMPITY-BUMP
IN A BLACKED OUT PLACE.
I MET HER
WITH A BUMPITY-BUMP
WITH A BUMPITY-BUMPITY-BUMP
IN THE BLACKOUT.

(*speaks in la-di-da English accent*) I say, Colonel, surely you can Bumpity-Bump better than that. What? Ha ha. Right, my darlings up there in the ashtrays, and us down here in the stalls. I have a lovely treat for you tonight, because you are going to sing for me Bumpity Bump. What are you going to sing? Bumpity Bump. I'd like to hear that on the count of two. One two—(*Gesture. No response from AUDIENCE.*) We're going to do much better than that, aren't we? I hope so. Right. Every time my friend the Colonel flashes his torch, you will sing Bumpity-

Bump. We'll have a little rehearsal. Come along, Colonel, give us a flash! (*ACTOR 1, as COLONEL in audience, gives a flash from his flash light.*)
(*sings*)
I MET HER WITH A ...
WITH A. ...
IN THE BLACKOUT.
MY HEART WENT
WITH A. ...
No, no, darlings. That will not do. Much more of that, and I shall leave the stage. I'm not doing this for the benefit of my health. I'm going to give you another crack at it. This time, the Maestro is going to waggle his stick. Can you see his stick? (*House lights on*) Good. Because you are going to sing Bumpity Bump whether you like it or not. Right. I'll have a flash from the Colonel and a waggle from the Maestro. (*MUSICAL DIRECTOR waves his baton.*) I can't offer you more than that, dears. Here we go. One two three four.
I MET HER
WITH A BUMPITY-BUMP,
WITH A BUMPITY-BUMP
IN THE BLACKOUT.
MY HEART WENT
WITH A BUMPITY-BUMP
WITH A BUMPITY-BUMP
IN THE BLACKOUT.

I PUT OUT MY LEFT HAND,
I PUT OUT MY RIGHT.
I FELT HER BUMPITY-BUMP
IN THE BLACKED OUT NIGHT.
I TURNED IN A CIRCLE,
I STUCK OUT MY FACE,
AND KISSED HER BUMPITY-BUMP
IN A BLACKED OUT PLACE.
(*House Lights off*)
I MET HER
WITH A BUMPITY-BUMP,
WITH A BUMPITY-BUMPITY-BUMP
IN THE BLACKOUT.

(*BLACKOUT. Table and chair set in blackout.*)

MARCH OF TIME. (*recorded voice*) December 7th, 1941. Pearl Harbor. America enters the war. February 12th, 1942. Moony Shapiro appointed liaison officer between British and American entertainment groups. June 21st, 1942. British forces surrender at Tobruk. Captain Shapiro captured and sent to prisoner of war camp, Germany.

(*Projection: POW Camp, Germany. BELLA is discovered at table, writing letter.*)

"DAS MADCHEN AM FENSTER" (*music only*)

BELLA. Darling Moony, Glad you got the socks and cake from the Red Cross. Do take care. I know how restless you get in one place . . . (*Exit BELLA with table and chair. MOONY and ACTOR 3 as PRISON GUARD enter, listening to song over camp radio.*)

GERMAN SOLDIERS CHORUS. (*recorded*)
ICH SEH' EIN MADCHEN AM FENSTER,
WIE BLUE AUGEN SIE HAT!
ICH BIN SOLDAT IN DER STRASSE,
HIER IN EIN SO FREMDER STADT.
LIEBE DICH,
LIEBE DICH,
HEIST DU VIELLEICHT
LORELEI?
LIEBST DU MICH?
LIEBST DU MICH?
ICH KOMM NOCH EINMAL
VORBEI!

MOONY. What's that they're singing, Fritz?

PRISON GUARD. It is a new song, Herr Kapitan. Das Mädchen Am Fenster. (*Projection fades.*)

MOONY. The Girl in the Window! I knew a commercial song when I heard one. Anyone can infringe a copyright. It's copyrighting the infringement that takes genius. I was into the escape tunnel like a flash—with my toothbrush, a photo of Bella, and a rough translation of the lyric.

(*Projection: New York skyline, day. Enter DA ROSA.*)

DA ROSA. Welcome home, soldier! Everyone's nuts about

your German song. Fifteen big records already, and a special launching tonight at the Stage Door Canteen by guess who? (*Lampost slides on.*)

MOONY. Who?

DA ROSA. You'll never guess!

(*Projection fades. Enter ACTRESS 1 as Marlene Dietrich in U.S. Army Uniform with rifle.*)

"THE GIRL IN THE WINDOW"

MARLENE DIETRICH.
I SAW A GIRL IN A WINDOW,
I SAW A GIRL LOOKING DOWN.
I NEARLY LET GO MY RIFLE
IN A STREET IN A FAR FOREIGN TOWN.
MARCHING BY
MARCHING BY
SHE WAVED AS I WENT MARCHING BY,
AND I PRAY
SHE WILL STAY
TILL I COME BACK THIS WAY
MARCHING BY . . .

MARCHING BY
MARCHING BY
SHE WAVED AS I WENT MARCHING BY,
AND I PRAY
SHE WILL STAY
TILL I COME BACK THIS WAY
MARCHING BY . . .

[FLY CUE: K] (*Exit MARLENE DIETRICH in one direction, the lampost in another. Projection: Victory Celebrations. Stage fills with Victory Flags. Enter COMPANY: ACTRESSES 1 & 2 in uniforms we have just seen them wearing; ACTOR 1 as British Army Officer; ACTOR 2 as American Army Officer; ACTOR 3 as U.S. SAILOR.*)

"VICTORY V" [MUSIC CUE 15]

COMPANY.
GIVE A ROUSIN' CHEER—HURRAH!
HAVE ANOTHER BEER—HURRAH!

ISN'T IT GREAT
TO CELEBRATE
WITH EVERYBODY HERE?
WHILE THOSE PLANES ARE WRITIN' IN THE SKY
V-I-C-T-O-R-Y !
LET'S PUT UP A V
FOR HAPPY VOICES,
AND LET'S GIVE 'EM AN I
FOR INDEPENDENCE,
C FOR ALL THE CHILDREN
WELCOMIN' THE BOYS BACK HOME.
LET'S PUT UP A T
FOR ALL THE TROOPSHIPS,
WHEN THEY'RE COMIN' BACK O
— VER ALL THE OCEANS,
R FOR THEIR RETURNING,
WITH A Y
FOR YOU-AND-ME,
WHILE THEY'RE RINGING OUT THE BELLS
ON THE HAPPY DAY THAT SPELLS
VICTORY V
VICTORY VICTORY V
YES, SIREE!

(*Exit ALL except ACTOR 1 who throws Army hat into wings and becomes STORYTELLER again. Projection changes from Victory Celebs to Hollywood.*) [FLY CUE: L]

STORYTELLER. Moony had had a good war, and was immediately snapped up by Hollywood — in the era of the great post-war musicals. He was at the height of his creative powers. Remember these Moony Shapiro evergreen? From "A Yank At The Vatican", starring Bing Crosby with Barry Fitzgerald as the Pope . . .

(*Enter ACTOR 3 as BING CROSBY.*)

"*APRIL IN WISCONSIN*" [MUSIC CUE 16]

WHEN IT'S APRIL IN WISCONSIN
AND I'M SITTIN' HERE IN ROME,
I AM LONGIN' FOR WISCONSIN
AND MY HUCKLEBERRY HOME.

ARE YOUNG MEADOWLARKS STILL SINGIN'?
IS THE SKY THE SAME OLD BLUE?
WHEN IT'S APRIL IN WISCONSIN,
AND YOUNG LOVERS HEARTS ARE DANCIN'
WHAT'S BECOME OF YOU?
DO YOU MISS ME?
IS THERE SOMEONE ELSE YOU'VE FOUND.
NOW IT'S SPRINGTIME?
YES, IT'S SPRINGTIME
WITH NEW LOVERS
AROUND.
BUT I PRAY THAT YOU'RE STILL WAITIN'
AND I'LL HEAR FROM YOU TODAY,
WHEN IT'S APRIL IN WISCONSIN
AND YOU'RE LOOKIN' SO ENTRANCIN'
FOUR THOUSAND MILES AWAY.

STORYTELLER. And who will ever forget Dan Dailey's memorable advice to the stage-struck kid in "Let's Do The Show Right Here"?

(*ACTOR 3 becomes DAN DAILEY.*)

"IT'S ONLY A SHOW" [MUSIC CUE 16A]

DAN DAILEY.
TRIUMPH AND DISASTER.
TREAT 'EM JUST THE SAME.
AND YOU WILL END UP BROADWAY'S NUMBER ONE.
IF YOU CAN KEEP YOUR HEAD
IN OBSCURITY AND FAME
YOU'LL BE A STAR, MY SON.

IF THE AUDIENCE CHEER
WHEN THE CURTAIN COMES DOWN,
AND THE CHAMPAGNE IS STARTIN' TO FLOW,
KID, YOU GOTTA REMEMBER—
IT'S ONLY A SHOW

IF YOU WAKE UP AND FIND
YOU'RE THE TOAST OF THE TOWN
AND YOU FEEL A SELF-SATISFIED GLOW.
FELLA, DON'T BE BIG-HEADED—
IT'S ONLY A SHOW.

STORYTELLER. (*continued*) Or the Mario Lanza title song from "Bring Back Tomorrow" . . .

(*ACTOR 3 becomes MARIO LANZA.*)

"*BRING BACK TOMORROW*" [MUSIC CUE 16B]   [WINCH CUE: 14]

MARIO LANZA.
BRING BACK TOMORROW
WHEN SKIES ARE NEVER GREY.
BRING BACK OUR YESTERDAYS
AND YESTERMONTHS
AND YESTERYEARS,
BE MINE TODAY . . .
(*Exit MARIO LANZA on final note. MOONY is at his piano which now has a mass of Oscars standing on it.*)

MOONY. (*sings*)
BRING BACK TO—
(*He cannot hit the high note so points upwards in the silence, swiftly dropping his arm for the last note.*)
—RROW.
My first Mario Lanza song.

STORYTELLER. These are just a few of his Oscars. For once Moony seemed prepared to settle down, but some bastards—HUAC, the House Unamerican Activities Committee and a certain Senator Joe McCarthy—from Wisconsin—just wouldn't let him. [MUSIC CUE 17] Bella and he, believe it or not, were branded dangerous Reds.

(*Enter COMPANY, as their first ACT I entrance, singing—*)

"*SONGBOOK*"

COMPANY.
HARD TIMES
NEED SOFT WORDS,
SWEET RHYMES
AND HUMMING B - - - -
(*They freeze, silent, mouths open.*)

STORYTELLER. Moony had seen it all. From silent movies to silent songs. In Hollywood, thanks to the madness of McCarthyism, he got no work for three years. During this interval— (*glances at gold watch*) I'm sure we could all use a drink.

CURTAIN

ACT TWO

[FLY CUE: A] *Entr'acte* [MUSIC CUE 18]. *The Curtain rises on ACTRESS 2 as BONNY VAN HEYSEN, perched high up in a cut-out hickory tree.* (preset) *She sings in a little girl voice. False legs dangle over the branches.*

"HAPPY HICKORY" [MUSIC CUE 19]

BONNY.
HI THERE, HAPPY HICKORY!
FOUR SQUARE, HAPPY HICKORY!
YOU'RE OUR MAGIC TREE,
SO WORK A MIRACLE PLEASE!
WORK A MIRACLE DO!
GRAND OLD HAPPY HICKORY,
YOU'RE GOLD, HAPPY HICKORY.
WHEN WE WISH ON YOU,
PLEASE HAPPY HICKORY TREE,
HAPPY HICKORY TREE,
MAKE IT—
HICKORY-DICKORY-DO!
—COME TRUE.

[FLY CUE: B] (*BONNY crosses the false legs to comic effect. Drop in silver cloth* DS. *of hickory tree. Enter STORYTELLER.*)

STORYTELLER. An eleven-year-old girl perched on a high branch of a magic hickory tree. That was the memorable sight and sound that greeted audiences as the curtain rose on Moony Shapiro's one important contribution to the American Music Theater, "Happy Hickory."

(*During speech MOONY has entered with table and chair, at which he sits—with writer's block.*)

MOONY. God, how I sweated for that show! A year of blank manuscript paper and full ashtrays. Would I ever get the damn score written? Bella had a suggestion.

(*Enter BELLA.*)

BELLA. Get off your ass!
MOONY. Thanks, Bella.
[FLY CUE: C] STORYTELLER. (*taking out letter*) A letter from Oscar Ham-

merstein the Second—(*reads*) Dear Moony, Bella's idea for a wishing tree musical is terrific. You have to do it. Put as much magic as you like in the show. We don't burn witches on Broadway. Not even for Senator McCarthy.

MOONY. God bless Oscar! I framed that letter. And resharpened my pencils for the fray. [WINCH CUE: 1]

BELLA. Darling, I know you'll be inspired at Pookie Van Heysen's. (*Fly out silver cloth. Projection: New England in Fall. MOONY goes to his white piano and sits at it.*)

MOONY. New England in October! Pookie's eleven-year-old daughter was my inspiration! Young Bonny was perfect for the top of the hickory tree. I had my director, Alvin Burns, fly up after I had written a tree-climbing song specially for Bonny.

(*Enter ACTOR 3 as ALVIN BURNS. BONNY skips on and sings.*)

"CLIMBIN'" [MUSIC CUE 20]

BONNY.
CLIMBIN' CLIMBIN'
I'M NOT AFEARED TO GO CLIMBIN'.
CHICKEN SCAREDY BABY,
HAVE A BIG RACE WITH ME
TO THE TOP OF THE TREE . . .
  MOONY. What d'ya think, Alvin?
  ALVIN. Bonny's terrific.
  MOONY. And the song?
  ALVIN. What song? Oh, that. No.
  MOONY. What d'ya mean, no?
  BONNY. What shall I do with the song, Moony?
  MOONY. You can keep it, kid. It's all yours.
  BONNY. Thank you. (*Exit ALVIN and BONNY.*)

BELLA. Darling, I think perhaps you'd be more inspired at Louis da Rosa's. (*Projection changes to Colorado in Winter.*)

MOONY. Colorado in November. Sun, snow, log fires—and a fantastic idea. I played the song for Louis.

(*Enter DA ROSA.*)

DA ROSA. Give me the scene.
MOONY. A village in the Appalachian Mountains called Pokenhatchit. The wicked Senator "Beanpole" Pickles is threat-

ening to cut down the magic wishing tree to make way for an eight-lane highway.

    Da Rosa. Strong stuff. I like it.

    Moony. Meanwhile our heroine, Rusty, sings the big song to her boyfriend—

"DON'T PLAY THAT LOVESONG ANY MORE"
[MUSIC CUE 20A]

DON'T SING THAT LOVESONG ANY MORE, MARVIN,
IT SENDS A SHIVER DOWN MY SPINE . . .
What d'ya think, Louis?

    Da Rosa. I'll say this for it.
    Moony. Yeh?
    Da Rosa. It's short.
    Moony. It develops.
    Da Rosa. Don't bother. Why d'you keep playing me that dreadful song?
    Moony. It's a great song!
    Bella. Darling, I think perhaps—

[FLY CUE: D]
    Da Rosa. Bella, I'll handle this. And I did. (*Exit BELLA.*)
    Moony. Jack Dempsey's basement in December!
    Da Rosa. I gave Moony the keys to a small basement room in New York, below the Brill Building. On December 25th, 1953. Merry Christmas! (*Exit. Fly in silver cloth.*)

[WINCH CUE: 2]
    Moony. Advice to budding show writers—travel shrinks the mind. A shoebox with inspiration is worth a dozen palaces. My Christmas lunch was pastrami and coleslaw. Songs poured out. I finished the score in fifteen days. The rest is history. You know, I still get a lump in the throat every time the curtain goes up on "Happy Hickory." (*Exit with table and chair.*)

[FLY CUE: E]
[FLY CUE: F]
    (*Fly out silver cloth. The hickory tree is in place again with a white fence slightly in front of it. Enter ACTRESS 1 as RUSTY, ACTOR 1 as MARVIN.* Note: *This musical is performed in the style of "Li'l Abner", "Finians Rainbow", and "Paint Your Wagon."*)

"HAPPY HICKORY" [MUSIC CUE 21]

    Rusty.
MARVIN BRENNAN, HAVE YOU MADE A WISH TODAY?

MARVIN.
IF I HAVE, WELL, I AIN'T TELLIN' YOU!

(*Enter ACTRESS 2 as JUDE, ACTOR 3 as CHUCK, ACTOR 2 as VILLAGER.*)

COMPANY.
HAPPY HICKORY, HAPPY HICKORY
MAKE IT COME TRUE . . . HM—HM—
HI THERE, HAPPY HICKORY!
FOUR SQUARE, HAPPY HICKORY!
YOU'RE OUR MAGIC TREE,
SO HAPPY HICKORY TREE,
HAPPY HICKORY TREE,
MAKE IT—
HICKORY-DICKORY-DO!
—COME TRUE.

(*RUSTY and MARVIN canoodle by fence. CHUCK and JUDE sing—*)

"LOVELY SUNDAY MORNIN'"

CHUCK.
ON SATURDAY NIGHT,
TO MY DELIGHT,
SHE STARTLED ME OUT OF MY WITS!
BOTH.
IT'S A LOVELY SUNDAY MORNIN' TODAY.
CHUCK.
AND ROUND ABOUT THREE,
SHE SAID TO ME—
JUDE.
I'M NOT A PERSON WHO QUITS.
BOTH.
IT'S A LOVELY SUNDAY MORNIN' TODAY.
THE RAIN'S POURIN' DOWN
ALL OVER THE TOWN,
AND EVERYTHING'S GLOOMY AND GREY,
CHUCK.
NOW I'VE GOT A GAL
WONDERFUL GAL
I'M GONNA LOVE HER TO BITS.

BOTH.
IT'S A LOVELY SUNDAY MORNIN',
FORGET THAT STORMY WEATHER WARNIN'
IT'S A LOVELY SUNDAY MORNIN'
TODAY.

(*CHUCK and JUDE swop places with RUSTY and MARVIN.*)

RUSTY. Gee, Marvin, you'll never guess what happened in bed last night?
MARVIN. Won't I, Rusty?
RUSTY. Heck, Marvin, I mean it—

"RUSTY'S DREAM BALLET"

RUSTY.
LAST NIGHT I HAD SUCH A DREAM, MARVIN.
IT WAS GOOD, MARVIN,
IN A WEIRD SORT OF WAY.
PEOPLE WERE DANCIN'
LEAPIN' AND PRANCIN' . . .
  MARVIN. Was I?
  RUSTY. You were!
  MARVIN. My!
  RUSTY.
YOU DANCED WITH ME IN MY DREAM, MARVIN.

LIKE A DREAM, MARVIN,
I'M HAPPY TO SAY.
  BOTH.
WE DANCED TOGETHER
AS LIGHT AS A FEATHER
IN RUSTY'S DREAM BALLET.

(*They dance together—CHUCK, JUDE, VILLAGER. Thunder and lightning. JUDE screams.* [MUSIC CUE 21A] *RUSTY and JUDE are sheltering under the Happy Hickory tree. MARVIN and CHUCK join them. The VILLAGER exits.*)

CHUCK. Hey, Jude, that's dangerous!
MARVIN. Shelterin' under a tree in a storm!

SONGBOOK 53

Jude. Not with you it ain't!

Rusty. Besides—it's a magic hickory tree. (*Thunder and lightning on cue.*)

"A STORM IN MY HEART"

Chuck.
YOU STARTED A STORM IN MY HEART
LIGHTNIN' HAS STRUCK ME TODAY . . .
Jude.
THERE'S SOMETHING SO WARM IN MY HEART
THE SUN IS SHININ' BRIGHTER
AND MY HEAD IS GROWIN' LIGHTER . . .
Marvin.
I FELT THAT TYPHOON PASSIN' THRU'
AND I WAS CARRIED AWAY . . .
Rusty.
HERE COMES THAT FULL MOON FOR US TWO
AFTER A STORM IN MY HEART.

(*The COUPLES kiss. Enter ACTOR 2 as the villainous SENATOR BEANPOLE PICKLES.*)

Beanpole. You kids won't be kissin' under that tree for long. It's comin' down to make way for my eight-lane highway. Sure as I'm Senator Beanpole Pickles.

Chuck. Hands off our town, Beanpole—and our magic hickory tree.

"POKENHATCHIT'S PUBLIC PROTEST COMMITTEE"
[music cue 21b]

Jude and Rusty.
WE'VE GOTTA STOP 'EM
D-D-D-D-D-D-DRILLIN'
WE GOTTA STOP 'EM
KILLIN' THIS TOWN,
WE NEED THE BODIES
ABLE AND WILLIN',
SO HURRY ON DOWN,
HURRY HURRY HURRY ON DOWN.

(*Throughout song JUDE, RUSTY, CHUCK & MARVIN advance menacingly on the retreating BEANPOLE.*)

ALL.
AND JOIN THE PEOPLE OF POKENHATCHIT'S PUBLIC PROTEST COMMITTEE,
PROTEST COMMITTEE,
PUBLIC PROTEST COMMITTEE,
SEND THAT SENATOR BEANPOLE PICKLES PACKIN' BACK TO THE CITY
WITH HIS TAIL A-DANGLE
HANGIN' BETWEEN HIS LEGS.
 CHUCK. Yup, we're gonna fix that polecat Senator real good!
ALL.
WE'LL BE KEEPIN' OUR POKENHATCHIT INDEPENDENT AND PRETTY,
WON'T IT BE PRETTY
WHEN THE GOIN' IS GRITTY,
AND THE PEOPLE OF POKENHATCHIT'S PUBLIC PROTEST COMMITTEE,
START TO TURN BACK THE TURNPIKE,
TURN BACK THE TURNPIKE,
SENATOR PICKLES,
SENATOR PICKLES,
SENATOR PICKLES
SENATOR PICKLES,
Please drop dead . . .

(*Flash of lightning. BEANPOLE, under tree, drops dead. MARVIN looks at him in astonishment, and steps over body.*)

 MARVIN. It was the tree that did it! I love you, Rusty!
 CHUCK. I love you, Jude!
 RUSTY & JUDE. We love you, Marvin and Chuck!
 ALL. Thanks to our magic Hickory Tree!

(*BEANPOLE springs to life and joins the Finale.*)

"HAPPY HICKORY"

 ALL.
HAPPY HICKORY
HAPPY HICKORY . . .

HI THERE, HAPPY HICKORY!
FOUR SQUARE, HAPPY HICKORY,
MAKE IT—
HICKORY DICKORY
HICKORY DICKORY
HICKORY DICKORY DO
COME TRUE!

(*Fly in silver cloth. ACTOR 1, throwing clothes into wings, resumes role of STORYTELLER, a touch out of breath.*) [FLY CUE: G]

STORYTELLER. (*humming*) Hi there, Happy Hickory! Four Square . . . What a show! Moony became a kind of cultural ambassador, whooping it up at productions of "HAPPY HICKORY" in London, Tokyo, Mexico City, Rome, Sydney . . . and Tel Aviv. (*Enter MOONY.*) [FLY CUE: H]

MOONY. 1956 was a particularly busy year. Abe and Minnie Shapiro—God rest their souls!—would have been proud of me. [MUSIC CUE 21C] We were in Israel for the show's ninth foreign production. It was a packed house. The opening number seemed great, although my knowledge of Hebrew was confined to the first line—

(*Projection: Israeli Flag. Enter ACTOR 3, ACTRESSES 1 & 2 wearing blue Israeli sun-hats. ACTOR 3 hands one to ACTOR 1.*)

"HAPPY HICKORY"

ACTRESSES 1 & 2, ACTORS 1 & 3.
SHALOM, HAPPY HICKORY,
SHALOM, HAPPY HICKORY.

MOONY. Something was wrong, however. (*SINGERS leave stage, one-by-one, looking concerned.*) The audience started leaving. It was a mass exodus! By the end of the first act, our chorus seemed much depleted, likewise the band, and no one at all was playing the part of Chuck. (*music out*) I dashed backstage to confront Producer Shmuel Levi. Doesn't *anybody* like it, Shmuel? What the hell's going on?

(*Enter ACTOR 3 as SHMUEL LEVI, carrying army hat.*)

SHMUEL. (*whisper*) Suez.

MOONY. (*bemused*) Who is?

(*Enter BELLA who joins MOONY.*)

SHMUEL. We are. Tomorrow. We have a little Sinai Campaign.
BELLA. Oh, I'm sorry.
MOONY. We didn't know.
SHMUEL. I know you didn't know. But now you know, I am arresting you for being in possession of secret information.
BELLA. Arresting us?!
SHMUEL. Yes, I am a Reserve Colonel of Security. (*puts on army hat*) So I order you to accept my hospitality. Come to my house. We will have something to drink. Maybe something to eat. Maybe play a little cards. Dance a hora. And then, maybe in the morning when the war starts, you can go. (*exit*) [MUSIC CUE 21D]

(*Projection changes to Hammer & Sickle with snow effect. Enter STORYTELLER in Russian winter coat and hat.*)

STORYTELLER. Moscow, a week later. After a gruesome journey, changing planes at Athens, Belgrade, and Budapest. The red carpet was out. Bella and Moony were sore from the official bearhugs, liverish from the caviar, and deaf from the sound of smashing glasses.
MOONY. Even in my crocked state, I was moved by the wonderful singing of the show's chorus—

(*Enter ACTOR 3 and ACTRESS 2 in Russian winter coats and hats. They join ACTOR 1.*)

"HAPPY HICKORY" (*in Russian*)

ZDRAST-VUY, HAPPY HICKORY!
ZDRAST-VUY, HAPPY HICKORY!

(*Exit ACTRESS 2 and ACTOR 3.*)

MOONY. Although I didn't understand a word, the rehearsals brought tears to my eyes. (*music out*)
BELLA. The monsters!
MOONY. Monsters? They're singing great!

BELLA. Fraternal friendship, my foot! (*Exit BELLA.*)

STORYTELLER. (*takes out Communique*) November 4th—Moscow radio—[MUSIC CUE 21E] (*reading*) "Soviet troops have crushed the forces of reactionary conspiracy among the Hungarian people, liquidating counter revolutionary gangs." (*end of reading*) The Western world was shocked by the callous Soviet brutality in Hungary. In protest the British cancelled a tour by the Sadlers Wells Ballet Company. The Russians cancelled "Happy Hickory." (*Music out, exit STORYTELLER.*)

MOONY. There was worse to come. Next day, Bella was late for lunch. Our bags were packed. We had a plane to catch. She said she'd only be an hour visiting an old friend. I waited and waited. At ten after three, I got a call. From the KGB.

(*Enter ACTRESS 2 as KGB.*)

KGB. We have some questions to ask you, Mr. Shapiro.

MOONY. Likewise. Where's my wife?

KGB. In the next room. What is your connection with Sacha Perelman?

MOONY. Never heard of her.

KGB. Him.

MOONY. Him.

KGB. Come now, Mister Shapiro, your wife visited the apartment this morning. Mister Perelman is a well-known anti-Communist.

MOONY. Look, can I call my Embassy, please?

KGB. What was your wife doing in Budapest on her way here? (*silence*) Did you know that she corresponds with many cosmopolitan pseudo-intellectuals? (*silence*) You are Jewish, Mister Shapiro, are you not?

MOONY. (*He shrugs to AUDIENCE. Then sings:*) [MUSIC CUE 21F]
SEATED ONE DAY IN THE KREMLIN
WHILE BANGING THE DESK WITH MY SHOE . . .
(*spoken*) That's all I remember of the "Nazi Party Pooper" rewrite I sent to Nikita Khruschev. But I still do have his reply. "Comrade Moony, I like the Hitler lyric better. P.S. When I come to America, could you arrange for me to meet Shirley Maclaine?"

(*Blackout. Projection: Broadway/Times Square Street sign. Enter STORYTELLER.*)

STORYTELLER. Moony's experiences of racial prejudice gave him an idea for a new musical, "Red White and Black," inspired by Emile Zola's "J'Accuse." In his version, Moony changed the Jewish Captain Dreyfus into the black Captain Robinson of the U.S. Army Air Force, wrongly court-martialled for selling secrets to the North Koreans. Broadway Producer-Director Harold Prince recalls—

(*Enter ACTOR 3 as HAROLD PRINCE, reading from book.*)

HAROLD PRINCE. I liked Moony a lot. He offered me "Red White and Black" but I had to turn it down because I was doing "West Side Story" at the time. We were all trying to make the American musical say more. But, frankly, I felt Moony was saying a bit too much. (*Exit HAROLD PRINCE.*)

[FLY CUE: I]

MOONY. "Red White and Black" opened with a Charity Premiere in Boston. The overture got a standing ovation. But for the rest of the performance, the audience sat on its hands. (*exit*)

[FLY CUE: J]

(*During following speech, fade projection and fly in Korean cloth. Enter ACTRESS 1 as KIM-SUNG, ACTRESS 2 as LIN-CHI on cue.*)

STORYTELLER. Unfortunately, there was no cast album. But the Shapiro estate has kindly provided Moony's original music and lyrics. And we would like to do a number from the show. When the Korean heroine, Kim-Sung, hears that her lover, Captain Robinson, has been condemned to be shot she meets her sister, Lin-Chi, And they sing—(*exit*)

[FLY CUE: K]

"I ACCUSE" [MUSIC CUE 22]

KIM-SUNG & LIN-CHI.
I ACCUSE
THE JUDGES OF PREJUDICE
IN THIS COURT MARTIAL.
I ACCUSE THE JUDGES OF UNFAIR PLAY,
NO WAY
IMPARTIAL.
OH AMERICA, AMERICA,
PLEASE DON'T TURN YOUR BACK
TO ONE LAW FOR THE WHITE
AND ANOTHER FOR THE BLACK . . .

IF THAT'S THE WAY YOU TREAT YOUR OWN,
HOW WILL YOU TREAT ME?
IF THAT'S THE WAY YOU TREAT YOUR OWN
THANK YOU FOR YOUR HERSHEY BARS,
FORD CARS,
CHEAP CIGARS—
YANKEE GO HOME!

IF YOU CAN DUMP YOUR FLESH-AND-BLOOD,
WHERE WILL YOU DUMP ME?
IF YOU CAN DUMP YOUR FLESH-AND-BLOOD,
THANK YOU FOR YOUR MOVIE QUEENS,
BLUE JEANS,
BENZEDRINES—
YANKEE GO HOME!

I USED TO THINK
THAT YOU WERE THE HAND THAT FED,
LAND THAT LEAD.
I USED TO THINK
THAT YOU WERE THE GREATEST THING
SINCE SLICED BREAD.

BUT
IF YOU CAN KILL YOUR KITH-AND-KIN,
WHEN WILL YOU KILL ME?
IF YOU CAN KILL YOUR KITH-AND-KIN,
THANK YOU FOR YOUR SHERMAN TANKS
BLOOD BANKS,
MANY THANKS!
(*gong*)
WHITE HOUSE,
MICKEY MOUSE . . .
(*gong*)
FALSE BREASTS
ATOM TESTS . . .
(*gong*)
LONG JOHNS,
PENTAGONS,
PX,
RUBBERNECKS,
FAIR PLAY,
CIA,

SCHLITZ BEER,
GONORRHEA—
YANKEE GO HOME!

[FLY CUE: L] (*BLACKOUT. Enter MOONY. He picks up music from trunk song pile.*)

MOONY. Tuxedo-ed Bostonians booed. Mink-wrapped matrons fled in outrage.

(*Enter STORYTELLER, carrying chair and news clipping.*)

STORYTELLER. Show-biz trade paper, "Variety," had the last word. (*reads clipping*)
"SHAPIRO PINKO CHINKO STINKO."
(*continues*) On the charred battlefield of Broadway, those connected with the show lost everything—wives, boyfriends, balls, hair, tables at Sardi's, and, most appalling loss of all, dollars.
MOONY. It was only a show! (*He scribbles on manuscript.*)
STORYTELLER. Said Moony, to anyone who would listen. But no one on Broadway would.
MOONY. My agent was always out. I could never catch a waiter's eye. Friends faded away like ghosts. And muggers crossed the street to avoid me. (*MOONY drops manuscript onto chair and exits. The STORYTELLER picks up manuscript, sits on chair, glances at manuscript, and sings the song.*)

"MESSAGES I" [MUSIC CUE 23]

STORYTELLER.
I'VE REALLY LEARNT MY LESSON
AND I SHOULD HAVE LEARNT BEFORE:
YOU MUST NEVER BE DEPRESSIN'
WITH A SONG THAT'S ANTI-WAR.
REMEMBER THAT A BLACK MAN
ALWAYS WEARS A MELON GRIN,
AND ONLY AS A BOXER DOES HE WIN,
AND NEVER KISSES LADIES WITH WHITE SKIN
MESSAGES,
MESSAGES,
MESSAGES ARE FOR WESTERN UNION.

LET TEACHERS DO THE TEACHIN',
LEAVE THE SOAPBOX TO THE SOAP.
AND THE SERMONS AND THE PREACHIN'
TO HIS HOLINESS THE POPE.

DON'T EVER KNOCK OUR PRESIDENT,
OR ROCK THE STATUS QUOS,
OR SATIRIZE OUR SPLENDID G.I. JOES
OR OTHERWISE YOUR BROADWAY SHOW WILL CLOSE.
MESSAGES,
MESSAGES,
MESSAGES ARE FOR WESTERN UNION.

DON'T BE A FREEDOM FIGHTER,
ONLY GIVE 'EM WHAT THEY LIKE.
THEY WOULD SHOOT A MOVIE-WRITER
MAKIN' DORIS DAY A DIKE.
AND DON'T SUGGEST THAT JOHN WAYNE
PLAY A SYMPATHETIC FAG,
'COS THAT'S A DESECRATION OF THE FLAG,
AND BLASPHEMY JUST AIN'T THE PUBLIC'S BAG.
MESSAGES,
MESSAGES,
MESSAGES ARE FOR WESTERN UNION.
MESSAGES,
MESSAGES,
MESSAGES ARE FOR WESTERN UNION.
MESSAGES.   [FLY
STORYTELLER. Moony always got it out of his system with a   CUE: M]
song. His trunk songs were extended graffiti set to music. (*Exit STORYTELLER with chair.*)

(*Projection: Bright Happy Birthday card. Enter MOONY and BELLA. Kids enter on cue: ACTOR 1 as LEE-PYONG-DO, ACTOR 3 as JOHNNY BAKUBA, ACTRESS 2 as MAGDA GYOR — the youngest. They carry parcels gift-wrapped.*)

MOONY. Around my 50th birthday, Bella decided we should put together something of a family. We adopted Magda Gyor from Budapest, Johnny Bakuba from Sharpville, and Lee Pyong-Do from Diem Bien Phu.

"HAPPY BIRTHDAY"

KIDS & BELLA.
HAPPY BIRTHDAY TO YOU,
HAPPY BIRTHDAY TO YOU,
HAPPY BIRTHDAY DEAR POPPA/MOONY
HAPPY BIRTHDAY TO YOU!
BELLA.
Come along, Johnny . . . (*JOHNNY is first to give his present to MOONY. MAGDA and LEE follow, and they swamp him with presents and kisses. MOONY breaks away, suddenly irritable.*)

MOONY. Christ, Bella, this is bedlam! How can I work with all these kids around? (*The KIDS exit, crying. MOONY is guilty about his outburst.*) Hey, you guys, has anyone seen my piano? [MUSIC CUE 23A]

(*Enter STORYTELLER.*)

STORYTELLER. Moony was not working on a new show, or even a new song. And fifty is a traumatic time to be idle. For nearly two years he became obsessed with his youthful preoccupation—

MOONY. It bothered me. Why no black notes between E and F, and B and C? Was there some metaphysical explanation? Perhaps a missing energy force in unknown sounds?

BELLA. Please, Moony, drop the science fiction and pick up the kids from school! (*Exit BELLA.*)

MOONY. Kids? Oh, yeh . . .

(*Projection changes to London Square.*)

STORYTELLER. Bella was becoming worried about her husband's crankiness. And New York a rough place to raise a family. Like many show business Americans they decided to move to London, England. (*press clipping*) From the London Daily Sketch, May 5th 1960. (*reads*) "Moony 'Happy Hickory' Shapiro and his wife, formerly Lady Klintoch, daughter of Chicago meat king, Paxton Rickenbacker, are furnishing their £50,000 Chester Square home." (*looking up from newspaper*) From his new London base, a songwriter in his sagging fifties set out to explore the Swinging Sixties. (*exit*)

MOONY. Bella got involved with Bertrand Russell and the Campaign for Nuclear Disarmament. I got sore feet, marching. And piles from sit-down protests against The Bomb. No time to write. Then 1963. News of a great new talent from the Newport Folk Festival. The times, they were a-changin'. [MUSIC CUE 24] Protest was now big money, messages in. I fixed up my bottom drawer song for Bob Dylan. (*exit*)

(*Enter ACTOR 3 as BOB DYLAN with guitar and mouth organ which he blows, to comic effect, at end of phrases.*)

"MESSAGES" II

THEY SING ON STOPPIN' KILLIN'
STOPPIN' BOMBIN' STOPPIN' WAR,
AND THE OUTLOOK'S PRETTY CHILLIN'
IF THE TREES DON'T GROW NO MORE.
THEY SING ABOUT POLLUTION
AND I TAKE THEIR POINT OF VIEW.
BUT I DON'T GET NO MESSAGES FROM YOU.
MESSAGES.
MESSAGES.
WHERE ARE THE MESSAGES FROM WESTERN UNION?

(*Exit BOB DYLAN. Enter STORYTELLER.*)

STORYTELLER. That was how the song figured in Moony's dreams. Unfortunately, Moony in no way figured in Dylan's dreams. As a Spokesman for Dylan so lucidly put it—

(*Enter ACTOR 3 as DYLAN SPOKESMAN, puffing joint.*)

DYLAN SPOKESMAN. Uh. Uh. . . . Uhhh . . . (*puffs*). Shit. (*Exit DYLAN SPOKESMAN.*)
STORYTELLER. For the first time in his life, Moony felt as though the Martians had landed.

(*Enter MOONY.*)

MOONY. Who are these kooks? Are we in the same business? On the same planet? Bella's nephew Benedict Rickenbacker came to see me in London. He was a rich young man with nothing better to do than try his luck with the British pop scene.

(*Enter ACTOR 3 as BENEDICT RICKENBACKER.*)

BENEDICT. The world's into youth, Uncle! Sinatra's finished. Groups are today's thing. With your money and my contacts, we'll happen. Chart-wise, you dig. (*Exit. Projection changes to Liverpool docks.*)
MOONY. I kinda dig. I squeezed into Benedict's M.G., and we sped north to the land of the new style song. Liverpool, after all those years! I couldn't resist a visit to St. Cecilia's Orphanage where I had spent my childhood. But the orphanage had been knocked down to make room for a maternity hospital. Which made me wonder whatever happened to Tilly, my childhood sweetheart, and that gold watch I gave her. (*Enter ACTRESS 2 as TILLY, now middle-aged.*) Have you still got it, Tilly?
TILLY. Yes, Michael.
MOONY. Michael? Nobody's called me that in forty years.
TILLY. 'Tis in my shoebox of memories.
MOONY. 'Twas the only thing I ever had from my father.
TILLY. I remember. (*Exit TILLY.*)
MOONY. To celebrate, Tilly cooked me a chip butty. A chip butty is a traditional Liverpool sandwich. Two thick slices of bread filled with Frenchfried potatoes. Very slimming (*exit*) (*Enter LIVERPOOL GROUP with Beatles wigs: ACTRESSES 1 & 2, ACTOR 3 and ACTOR 1 as Drummer like Ringo Starr.*) Benedict's group was rehearsing in the basement of a crumbling Georgian mansion. I spoke to them in the local dialect. Hullo, wackers. I just ate a grotty chip butty for me dinner.
MEMBER OF GROUP. (*ACTOR 3*) Are you tryin' to be funny?
MOONY. I was born here!
MEMBER OF GROUP. (*ACTOR 3*) Who was on the throne? King Arthur? (*The GROUP sing, and ACTOR 1 plays drums to comic effect.*)

[WINCH CUE: 3]

"I FOUND LOVE" [MUSIC CUE 25]

ACTOR 3. (*like John Lennon*)	ACTRESSES 1 & 2.
I FOUND LOVE	I FOUND LOVE
AND I RECKON THAT YOU FOUND LOVE	

WE'VE A HECK OF A NEW FOUND LOVE	
WE FOUND LOVE	WE FOUND LOVE
ONE MORE	ONE MORE TIME
YOU WERE EAGER TO HOLD MY HAND	OO------
IT WAS GETTING SO COLD MY HAND	OO------
WE FOUND LOVE AT THE BACK OF THE CHURCH-YARD	WE FOUND LOVE OO------
DON'T COST A PENNY WHAT WE DID	OO------
DON'T TELL YOUR MOTHER OR YOUR DAD	OO------
DON'T GIVE A THOUGHT TO YESTERDAY	OO------
NO NO NO	NO NO NO
YESTERDAY'S BAD	
YEH YEH BAD	YEH YEH BAD
OO------	OO------
I FOUND LOVE	I FOUND LOVE
AND I RECKON THAT YOU FOUND LOVE	
WE'VE A HECK OF A NEW FOUND LOVE	
WE FOUND LOVE	WE FOUND LOVE
YEH YEH LOVE	YEH YEH LOVE
WE FOUND LOVE	WE FOUND LOVE
YEH	YEH
YEH	YEH
I FOUND LOVE	I
LOVE YEH YEH YEH	LOVE
I FOUND LOVE	I
LOVE YEH YEH YEH	LOVE
YEH	YEH
YEH	YEH
YEH	YEH

(*Projection fades. Exit GROUP, except ACTOR 1 who tears off wig and becomes STORYTELLER again.*)   [WINCH CUE: 4]

STORYTELLER. A hit! A hit! A palpable hit! Thousands of screaming girls mobbed the record shops. But where was the record? Unfortunately, young Benedict had pushed Moony into buying their own record company.

(*Enter MOONY and BELLA. Projection: Big Ben, London.*)

BELLA. What do you know about industrial relations, Moony? You know the British won't work without their tea break.
MOONY. Bella was right. The workers struck. I negotiated. I was tough but fair-minded.

(*Enter ACTOR 3 as TRADES UNION LEADER.*)

TRADES UNION LEADER. As chairman of the joint shop steward's committee, I'm here to inform you that we must have a ten-minute break.
MOONY. Eight.
TRADES UNION LEADER. Ten.
MOONY. Nine.
TRADES UNION LEADER. Ten.
MOONY. Eleven.
TRADES UNION LEADER. Twelve.
MOONY. Done. (*shakes hands with TRADES UNION LEADER who exits*) But by the time it was settled and the record in the shops, the fans had moved on—to another Liverpool Sound.
STORYTELLER. In 1964 he opened a discotheque on a Thames riverboat. It sank.
MOONY. I was scuttled.
STORYTELLER. In 1965, he missed the boat again—with a song called "Uptown." Unfortunately, record fans that year were all going in the opposite direction. So that sank, too.
MOONY. I've had it. Let's try Australia.
BELLA. Emigrate? Again? We're getting too old for that sort of thing.
MOONY. Speak for yourself.
BELLA. Thank you. (*a pause*) If you can spare a moment, Johnny wants a word with you.

(*Enter ACTOR 3 as JOHNNY BAKUBA, a young man now.*)

MOONY. Johnny who?
BELLA. Your son! (*exit*)
JOHNNY. Dad, I'm taking Holy Orders.
MOONY. Put me down for half a dozen.
JOHNNY. I'm going into the Church. (*exit*)
MOONY. Mazeltov! Let's drink to that.

STORYTELLER. And now we come to an incident only lightly touched upon in Moony's autobiography. The affair with Bonny Van Heysen. Remember her? The family friend. The little girl on top of the "Happy Hickory" tree. (*imitates song and dance*) Climbin' . . . Climbin' . . . Bonny was now twenty-four. On her way back from seeing her guru in India, drop-out Bonny decided to drop back in — on Moony.

(*Enter BONNY.*)

BONNY. Guru says I should be a pop star.

MOONY. A pop star? They're babies today. Aren't you a little old for that?

BONNY. Guru says we're all getting older, Moony.

MOONY. A pop star. Why not? I'll manage you. We'll call you . . . Bonny Brown.

BONNY. Far out! Bonny Brown, I love it, I love it! [MUSIC CUE 25A]

STORYTELLER. For Moony, London swung again. All in the cause of Bonny Brown. Strutting down the King's Road like a peacock in paradise, he sported a Carnaby Street shirt open to the navel, only occasionally staggering under the weight of his dangling medallions. (*exit*) (*BONNY kisses MOONY. They go their separate way. Projection changes to London Square at night.*) [WINCH CUE: 5]

MOONY. I came home late one night. Bella was not in bed. She had been going through my music and had dug out an old song of mine. (*Enter BELLA. She picks up music from trunk song pile, and sits at piano.*) It was one of the only times I ever heard her sing.

"DON'T PLAY THAT LOVESONG ANY MORE, SAM"
[MUSIC CUE 26]

BELLA. (*picks out notes on piano, then sings*)
DON'T PLAY THAT LOVESONG ANY MORE, SAM,

IT SENDS A SHIVER DOWN MY SPINE.
AND IF YOU WANT TO KNOW THE SCORE, SAM,
THE ONE I LOVE'S NO LONGER MINE.
WE'VE HAD OUR VERY LAST ENCORE, SAM.
IT WASN'T LIKE IT USED TO BE.
DON'T PLAY THAT LOVESONG ANY MORE, SAM.
NOT FOR ME.

FUNNY HOW A NUMBER
FROM SOME OLD BROADWAY SHOW
CONJURS UP A PLACE, A FACE, A SMILE.
FUNNY HOW THAT MUSIC
WE DANCED TO LONG AGO
HAD A HAPPY RING, A SWING, A STYLE.
BUT FASHIONS CHANGE.
AND PASSIONS CHANGE . . .

DON'T PLAY THAT LOVESONG ANY MORE, SAM,
IT FOLLOWS ME ALL OVER TOWN.
THAT MUSIC GETS ME ON THE RAW, SAM.
THE ONE I LOVE HAS LET ME DOWN.

SO THIS IS ALL I'M ASKING FOR, SAM—
PLAY ANY OTHER MELODY!
DON'T PLAY THAT LOVESONG ANY MORE, SAM,
NOT FOR ME.

MOONY. The song that nobody wanted . . .

BELLA. Why didn't they?

MOONY. I dunno. It was always rejected. (*MOONY has touched a sore point with BELLA.*)

BELLA. D'you know what time it is? (*MOONY shrugs.*) Buy a watch.

MOONY. I don't use 'em.

BELLA. It's about time you got over that.

MOONY. It's alright for you. You knew your father.

BELLA. Old sonofabitch. I'd have swopped him for a watch any day. Where 've you been?

MOONY. Annabel's.

BELLA. With Bonny?

MOONY. I have to promote her, darling. Anyway, she's a family friend. What harm can it do? (*BELLA walks slowly offstage. Projection fades. Enter STORYTELLER with press clipping.*)

STORYTELLER. From the Daily Express, March 10th, 1972. (*reads*) "Mrs. Moony Shapiro, formerly Lady Klintoch, daughter of Chicago meat king, Paxton Rickenbacker, is on her way north to organize mass demonstrations against the Polaris missile base at Holy Loch, Scotland. (*BELLA enters, setting up table and chair.*) Meanwhile, back in London, husband Moony continues to campaign for the sultry Bonny Brown, his perennial Pop Protegee. 'I just love his songs' Bonny told me, 'The old songs are the best'" (*puts down press clipping*) A letter from Bella to Moony—(*BELLA sits at table and writes.*)

BELLA. (*writing letter*) Darling Old Fool, Cheating on me in public is in the worst possible taste. Scotland still gets the London papers, you know.

STORYTELLER. A letter from Magda to Moony.

MOONY. (*reading letter*) Dear Daddy. If you want to know, you're being bloody embarrassing.

STORYTELLER. A letter from Johnny to Moony—

MOONY. (*reading letter*) Dear Dad. Sometimes I wish I were not your son. Praying for you every night.

STORYTELLER. A letter from Bella to Moony.

BELLA. (*writing letter*) Dear Moony. I've torn up four begging letters and got angrier at each cliché. Stop banging that girl. End of cliché.

STORYTELLER. A letter from Bonny to Moony—

(*Enter BONNY.*)

BONNY. Amazing Moonbug! What a fantastic time we've had. I really, really mean it. Introducing me to Benedict Rickenbacker and helping me clinch the EMI deal have been the two most wonderful things that have ever happened to me. We're off to LA to finish the album. Sorry. But you *did* say, once, I should find a younger fella. Love, Bonny. (*exit*)

STORYTELLER. A letter from Bella to Moony—

BELLA. Eight pages on the loss of your bitch is very boring. When I have completed my work at Holy Loch, I will be coming back to London. But not, I'm afraid, to you. [MUSIC CUE 27] (*Exit BELLA and STORYTELLER taking table and chair. MOONY puts on old bath-robe, goes to piano and takes swig from his hip-flask.*)

MOONY. So there I was, totally alone, at sixty-four. My only contact with Scotland was a bottle of Johnny Walker. (*MOONY takes a song from the trunk song pile and sings—.*)

"GOLDEN OLDIE"

Moony.
THEY SAY YOU'RE WORN OUT
GOLDEN OLDIE.
IS YOUR HEART TORN OUT,
GOLDEN OLDIE?
WELL, HERE'S THEIR ANSWER—
MY HEART STILL HAS A BEAT,
MY TEETH ARE NEARLY COMPLETE,
AND I CAN STAND ON MY FEET
WITHOUT TWO CRUTCHES.
HOPE SPRINGS ETERNAL
WITHOUT DIMMIN',
FORGET THE DIETS
AND THE SLIMMIN'.
IN NEXT TO NO TIME,
YOU'LL BE MAKIN' YOUR MARK WITH THE WOMEN,
GOLDEN OLDIE
ONE MORE TIME.

GOLDEN OLDIE,
OLD AN' MOLDY,
EVERYONE PUTS ME ON THE SHELF,
NOBODY PLAYS ME BUT MYSELF.
NO ONE CAN STRIKE ME OFF THE LIST.
I'M GONNA SHOW 'EM I EXIST!

THEY'RE GONNA MISS YOU,
GOLDEN OLDIE.
THEY'LL SOON RE-ISSUE
GOLDEN OLDIE.
THEY SAY YOU'RE FINISHED—
WHAT THE HELL DOES IT PROVE?
IF I CAN KEEP ON THE MOVE,
I'LL BE RIGHT BACK IN THE GROOVE
WITH ALL THE FAN CLUB.
'COS WHEN YOU MAKE THAT
NEW BEGINNING,
YOU'LL BE THE LOSER
WHO IS WINNING.
BEFORE YOU KNOW IT,

THAT IMPOSSIBLE WORLD WILL BE SPINNING,
GOLDEN OLDIE,
ONE MORE TIME.
(*exit*)

(*Enter STORYTELLER.*) [WINCH CUE: 6]

STORYTELLER. Moony, as always, was bouncing back. He had a deadline to meet with his autobiography, "Moon In June." He thought he had written the last chapter, but there was yet another twist to the Shapiro saga on that week's Ed Sullivan Show. Remember the tree-climbing song Moony wrote for young Bonny? (*imitation of BONNY*) Climbin', Climbin, I'm not afeared to go Climbin' . . . (*normal voice*) Well, she'd come a long way since then, climbin' up the record charts as Bonny Brown—and the Climbers.

(*Enter BONNY with her lead singer, ACTOR 3 as CLYDE, and ACTRESSES 1 & 2, ACTORS 1 & 2 as Backing Group. All wear Afro wigs.*)

"*CLIMBIN'*" [MUSIC CUE 28]
BONNY AND CLIMBERS. (*in Tamla Motown style*)
LET'S GO CLIMBIN'
LET'S GO CLIMBIN'
LET'S GO CLIMBIN'
LET'S GO CLIMBIN'
CLIMBIN' CLIMBIN' CLIMBIN' CLIMBIN'
UP TO THE TOP

LET'S GO CLIMBIN'
CLIMBIN' CLIMBIN'
HAH! YAH!
OOO----- OOO-----
OOO----- OOO-----
HIGHER! HIGHER!
CLIMBIN' TO THE TOP!
COME CLIMB WITH ME
TO THE TOP OF THE TREE

CLIMBIN' CLIMBIN'
HAH! YAH!

OOO----- OOO-----
OOO----- OOO-----
HIGHER! HIGHER!
CLIMBIN' TO THE TOP!
COME CLIMB WITH ME
TO THE TOP OF THE TREE
   Bonny.
CLIMBIN'
OOO-----
CLIMBIN'
I'M NOT AFRAID TO GO CLIMBIN'
CHICKEN, SCAREDY BABY
COME CLIMB WITH ME
TO THE TOP OF THE TREE
HOO! ------
   Bonny/Clyde.
HIGHER
AND HIGHER
   Bonny.
THERE'S A NEW WORLD TO ADMIRE   Climbers.
HIGHER ------
OOO-----   OOO-----
TAKE A FLIER

   HIGHER

AND IN NO TIME
YOU'LL FIND
   Bonny/Clyde.
I'LL BE BLOWIN' YOUR MIND   AH-----
LET'S GO   LET'S GO
CLIMBIN' CLIMBIN'

   HAH! YAH!

OOO----- OOO-----
OOO----- OOO-----
HIGHER HIGHER

   CLIMBIN' TO THE
COME CLIMB WITH ME   TOP
TO THE TOP OF THE TREE
CLIMBIN' CLIMBIN'

   HAH! YAH!

OOO----- OOO-----
OOO----- OOO-----
HIGHER HIGHER

COME CLIMB WITH ME
TO THE TOP OF THE TREE
  BONNY.
CLIMB UP CLIMB
UP THE TREE
 	
YOU WON'T CLIMB OVER ME
-------- AND WE'LL
BE BREAKIN' FREE
CLIMBIN' CLIMBIN' HIGHER
YOU AND ME
 	
CLIMB HIGHER
 	
I'M HIGHER
  BONNY/CLYDE.
WE'RE GONNA MAKE IT
BABY GONNA MAKE IT
  ALL.
BABY GONNA MAKE IT
LET'S GO CLIMBIN'
LET'S GO CLIMBIN'
LET'S GO CLIMBIN'
LET'S GO CLIMBIN'
  BONNY/CLYDE.
CLIMBIN'
 	
CLIMBIN'
 	
CLIMBIN'
 	
  BONNY.
I'M
 	
I'M
	CLIMBIN' TO THE
	TOP
	
	CLIMBIN'
	
	OOO-----
	CLIMBIN'
	
	OOO-----
	OOO-----
	CLIMB' ---
	-IN' -----
	HIGHER
	
	OOO----- HIGHER

(continued right column bottom)

HIGHER

HIGHER

HIGHER
  CLIMBIN'
HIGHER
  CLIMBIN'
HIGHER
  CLIMBIN'
HIGHER

    BONNY/CLYDE.
    CLIMBIN'   HIGHER

SONGBOOK

CLIMBIN'
              HIGHER
WE'RE
CLIMBIN' --------

(*Exit BONNY and the CLIMBERS, except ACTOR 1 who tears off Afro wig and becomes STORYTELLER again.*)

STORYTELLER. "Climbin'" climbed to Number One. And that was the beginning of Moony Shapiro, Cult Figure. The nostalgia of the early Seventies created a new interest in his old material. Bob Dylan hit Number 3 with "Messages." "Happy Hickory" was revived with an all-black cast, and retitled "The Hickey." This brought him quite a new little fortune.

(*Enter MOONY and BELLA. MOONY walks with a cane, a book under his arm.*)

MOONY. But the best fortune of all was my reconciliation with Bella.
BELLA. So we owe it all to Bonny!
MOONY. To think—I gave her that song.
BELLA. Kept it in her panties, dear. Or doesn't she wear 'em?
MOONY. I forget.
BELLA. You are a seedy old thing, darling.

(*Projection: Remote Irish cottage.*)

STORYTELLER. Bella and Moony settled in a farmhouse near Skibbereen, in Ireland. Bella got into organic farming and ecology, and wouldn't let anything pass their lips that had not grown naturally in the soil.
BELLA. No lobster, Moony. No steak. Not even a pork sausage.
MOONY. (*opens book*) It was the nearest I had been to a Kosher diet since my early New York days. And here I was in Skibbereen, Ireland. Not a bad full circle for a Liverpool Irish orphan with United States citizenship and a Jewish surname. (*closes book*) Well, folks, we've celebrated the past. Memory Lane is a fun place, but I could never live there permanently. Nostalgia is not my style. Me, I'm looking forward—to my next song. (*Exit MOONY.*)

STORYTELLER. Those were the closing words of "Moon in June," published by Doubleday in 1976. So you'll have to rely on me to complete Moony's songbook. We've compiled, with the help of his widow, Mrs. Arabella Shapiro, formerly Lady Klintoch, etcetera, a reconstruction of his extraordinary last days. [MUSIC CUE 28A]

BELLA. My husband became totally obsessed with his search for the missing black notes between E and F, and B and C. (*A cacophony of unusual antique and electronic musical instruments.*) He locked himself away for hours. The sounds got weirder and weirder.

STORYTELLER. But on September 6th, 1977, the sounds stopped. (*The sounds stop.*) There was a power cut in Skibbereen. And in New York, the lights went out on Broadway. Coincidence? Or something stranger?

BELLA. Moony was found dead in his studio, apparently electrocuted by a synthesizer. (*Exit. STORYTELLER takes music from trunk song pile.*) [WINCH CUE: 7]

STORYTELLER. And for the first time on any stage, ladies and gentlemen, we are privileged to bring you—by kind permission of the Shapiro estate—Moony's last song. Which I personally believe to be one of his most—(*searching for adjective*)—oh, why don't I just sing it for you—(*A straw hat and cane are thrown to STORYTELLER from opposite wings.*)

"NOSTALGIA" [MUSIC CUE 29]

STORYTELLER.
NOSTALGIA
IS YOUR TIFFANY LAMPS.
NOSTALGIA
IS YOUR JEAN HARLOW VAMPS.
AS FOR ME
I REMEMBER THE FREIGHT TRAIN RIDES,
THE GRAPES OF WRATH,
THE WALL STREET CRASH,
AND THE SUICIDES.

THE THIRTIES
DID HAVE MUSIC BY COLE,
AND GERTIE'S
GAY CAVORTING WITH NOEL.

OH WHAT FUN
WHEN YOU'RE WALKING DOWN MEM'RY LANE,
BUT THAT INCLUDES
THE BOMBS THEY DROPPED
IN THE WAR IN SPAIN.

WHICH GOOD OLD DAYS
WERE GOOD FOR WHO?
FOR SOME TERRIFIC
FOR SOME POOR BUMS
BOO-HOO!

NOSTALGIA
IS THE VOICE OF ASTAIRE.
NOSTALGIA
IS A FULL HEAD OF HAIR.
SING THE BLUES
FOR THE TWENTIETH CENTUR-EE,
THE GOLDWYN FOLLIES,
BEGINNING OF SWING,
AND TEDDIE AND WALLIS
DOING THEIR THING,
'COS MUCH MUCH WORSE WAS HAPPENING
NOSTALGIA'S NOT FOR ME

(*Music continues. Enter ACTRESS 1 as SHEILA O'TOOLE.*)

IRISH TIMES. Sheila O'Toole, Irish Times. The eulogy was read in Cork Cathedral by the deceased's son, Bishop John Bakuba Shapiro. (*Exit.*)

(*Enter JOHNNY. The STORYTELLER dances. Meanwhile—*)

JOHNNY. As the adopted son of a fatherless father, I know what my father was searching for. A place he belonged. He never quite found it, but he certainly made the most of the journey.... (*The STORYTELLER continues to sing.*)

[WINCH CUE: 8]

STORYTELLER.
DID SUMMERS
ALL HAVE PERMANENT SUN,
WHEN SLUMMERS
WENT TO HARLEM FOR FUN?

FURTHER SOUTH
I REMEMBER THE FUN BEGAN
WHEN FOLK PUT ON
THEIR CHIC WHITE HOODS
FOR THE KU KLUX KLAN.

WHICH GOOD OLD DAYS
WERE GOOD FOR WHO?
FOR SOME TERRIFIC
FOR SOME POOR BUMS
BOO-HOO!

NOSTALGIA
KEEPS YOU COZY AND WARM
NOSTALGIA
IS AN OLD UNIFORM.
PARDON ME,
IF THE MEMORIES KILL MY SMILE
THE ANGELS DINING
AT EV'RY DAMN RITZ,
THE SILVERY LINING
AFTER THE BLITZ.
THE BRAVE NEW WORLD
WE BLEW TO BITS!
NOSTALGIA'S NOT MY STYLE.
JUST TO SUM IT UP EVERYBODY—
NOSTALGIA'S NOT MY STYLE.
(*spoken*) Well's that's about it. Except—[MUSIC CUE 30] (*twirls the gold watch*)—this watch. Moony got it from his mother, who got it from his father—for services rendered. How did I get it?

(*Projection: Liverpool Docks. Flashback to earlier scene: young MOONY and TILLY.*)

TILLY. Oh, sweetheart, I'll never see you again!
MOONY. Tilly, take this—(*He gives her his gold watch.*)—to remember me by.
TILLY. But it was your mum's!
MOONY. It'll bring you luck. (*He kisses her. They exit. Projection fades.*)

STORYTELLER. That's how I got it. From my mother. Tilly. And all I got from my father was . . . (*taking out manuscript from his pocket*)

(*Projection: Gold Disc.*)

"DON'T PLAY THAT LOVESONG ANY MORE"

STORYTELLER.
DON'T PLAY THAT LOVESONG ANY MORE, SAM,
IT SENDS A SHIVER DOWN MY SPINE,
AND IF YOU WANT TO KNOW THE SCORE, SAM,
THE ONE I LOVE'S NO LONGER MINE.

(*Enter rest of COMPANY.*)

COMPANY.
WE'VE HAD OUR VERY LAST ENCORE, SAM,
IT WASN'T LIKE IT USED TO BE.
DON'T PLAY THAT LOVESONG ANY MORE, SAM,
NOT FOR ME,
NOT FOR ME.

(*Projection changes to SONGBOOK logo for curtain calls.*)

"SONGBOOK"

I'VE GOT A
SONGBOOK
IN MY HAND,
AND NOW IT'S
ON THE PIANO STAND,
I'LL PLAY A HAPPY SONG FROM MY
SONGBOOK,
SONGBOOK . . .

DOWN DAYS
NEED UPBEATS,
ALWAYS
MY HEART REPEATS—

KILL THAT WORRIED LOOK

WITH A SONGBOOK
WITH A SONGBOOK
WITH A SONG
FROM YOUR SONGBOOK,

[MUSIC CUE 31 — "EXIT MUSIC".]

    CURTAIN

FLY CUES

ACT ONE

Transitions:

A	FOLLIES sign IN on Direct Cue
B	Glame IN—together on Direct Cue Blackout Drop IN
C	*CLOSED CHANGE—NOT CUED* East River Drop IN
D	FOLLIES Sign OUT on Direct Cue
E	Glame OUT—together on Direct Cue Blackout Drop OUT
F	Glame IN—On Direct Cue
G	*CLOSED CHANGE—NOT CUED* East River Drop OUT
H	Glame OUT—On Direct Cue
I	Les Halles IN—on Direct Cue
J	Les Halles Drop OUT—on Direct Cue
K	Victory V Sign IN—on Direct Cue
L	Victory V Sign OUT—on Direct Cue

NOTE: Lampost pulled offstage during *Girl in the Window*—on Direct Cue.

ACT TWO

Transitions:

Preset:	Tree hanging in	Tree onstage
	Hickory drop in	
	Blackout drop in	
A	Blackout drop out on DIRECT CUE	
B	Blackout drop in on DIRECT CUE *CLOSED CHANGE—NOT CUED* Tree hanging out—Tree offstage	

SONGBOOK

C Hickory drop out
   Blackout drop out — together on DIRECT CUE

D Hickory drop in
   Blackout drop in — together on DIRECT CUE
   CLOSED CHANGE — NOT CUED
   Tree hanging in — Tree onstage (Fences on)

E Blackout drop out on DIRECT CUE

F Hickory drop out on DIRECT CUE

G Hickory drop in
   Blackout drop in — together on DIRECT CUE
   CLOSED CHANGE — NOT CUED
   Tree hanging out — Tree offstage (Fences off)

H Hickory drop out
   Blackout drop out — together on DIRECT CUE

I Glame in
   Blackout drop out — together in DIRECT CUE
   CLOSED CHANGE — NOT CUED
   Korean drop in — Korean lantern set

J Blackout drop out on DIRECT CUE

K Glame out on DIRECT CUE

L Blackout drop in on DIRECT CUE —
   Strike Korean lantern
   CLOSED CHANGE — NOT CUED
   Korean drop out

M Blackout drop out on DIRECT CUE

WINCH MOVES

ACT ONE

Transitions:

Preset	Stage Right	Piano to 1st position – direct cue
1.	Stage Right	Piano to 2nd position – direct cue
2.	Stage Right	Piano off – direct cue
3.	Stage Left	Upright Piano on – direct cue
4.	Stage Left	Upright Piano off – direct cue
5.	Stage Left	Upright Piano on – direct cue
6.	Stage Left	Piano off – direct cue
7.	Stage Left	Upright Piano on – direct cue
8.	Stage Left	Upright Piano off – direct cue
9.	Stage Right	Piano to 1st position – direct cue
10.	Stage Right	Piano to 2nd position – direct cue
11.	Stage Right	Piano off – direct cue
12.	Stage Right	Piano to 1st position – direct cue
13.	Stage Right	Piano off – direct cue
14.	Stage Right	Piano to 2nd position – direct cue

ACT TWO

Preset:	Stage Right	Piano off – Drum Wagon off Stage Left
1.	Stage Right	Piano to 1st Position – closed change
2.	Stage Right	Piano off – closed change
3.	Stage Left	Drum Wagon on to center – direct cue
4.	Stage Left	Drum Wagon off – direct cue
5.	Stage Right	Piano to 1st position – direct cue
6.	Stage Right	Piano off – direct cue
7.	Stage Right	Piano to 2nd position – direct cue
8.	Stage Right	Piano to 1st position – direct cue

PROJECTION SLIDES*

ACT ONE

Songbook	9
Liverpool Docks	13
Statue of Liberty	14
Palm Tree	21
Times Square	22
Statue of Liberty (Black & White)	24
New York Skyline Night	25
Eiffel Tower, Paris	27
Gare de Lyon	29
Olympics Insignia	33
Plaza Hotel, New York	35
Central Park, New York	38
Big Band	39
Big Ben, London	40
Victory Celebrations	44
Hollywood	45

ACT TWO

New England in Fall	49
Colorado in Winter	49
Israeli Flag	55
Hammer & Sickle with snow effect	56
Broadway/Times Square street sign	57
Happy Birthday Card	61
London Square	62
Liverpool Docks	64
Big Ben, London	66
London Square Night	67
Remote Irish Cottage	74
Liverpool Docks	77
Gold Disc	78

---

*Slides are a simplified list of those used in the original production. Their use is optional at the discretion of subsequent producers. SAMUEL FRENCH, INC. does not have the original slides available.

PROPS

ACT ONE

Stage Left

Trunk—Down Left—"in one"—In Trunk:
  First Drawer:
    Metronome
    Rhyming dictionary
    Hip flask
    Army hat
  Second Drawer:
    Manuscript music including
    1-MEG
    2-NAZI PARTY POOPER
    3-MESSAGES I
    4-DON'T PLAY THAT LOVESONG ANYMORE
    5-GOLDEN OLDIE
    6-NOSTALGIA
    Plus extra padding, all tied with a red ribbon
    APRIL IN WISCONSIN—printed
Upright piano with bench
Preset with shawl and Menorah, rosary & cross
Dust cloth—Mrs. Shapiro
"THE HAPPY HOOFER" (Book)
Silver straw hat for Actor 3.
Laundry basket for Mrs. Kleinberg
Laundry ticket for Mr. Wu
Luggage for M/M Shapiro
Clipboard with press clipping for Immigration Officer
New York Time picture—on upright
Canvas Director's chair with Hollywood newspaper "Major Star Weds Minor Musician"
Big cigar with fake light—handkerchief—for Da Rosa
Gold megaphone
Cigarettes and stick matches for Moony
Cigar for Moony
Live 1930's mike for JE VOUS AIME—cigarette and lighter—for Actor 1
Press clipping—Dolly ("Is it red roses for a Red Lady?")

SONGBOOK

Sling for Bella with pencil
Basket of flowers—LES HALLES
Book—Goebbel's DIARIES
NBC mike for Dolly
Radio script for Dolly ("Hi there. Here's Dolly Ralston . . .")
Flashlight for BUMPITY-BUMP
Letter from Bella—for Moony
German rifle for Fritz
Pipe—Bing Crosby for Actor 3.
Table and two chairs

Stage Right

Grand Piano—preset at center
Songbook sheet music on downstage edge of piano
"Moon In June" (Book) on piano
Gold watch on piano
Silver straw hat for Actor 1. (Actress 2)
Handbag for Mrs. Shapiro
Cloth cap & carpetbag for Moony
Mary Cassidy's broom
Rocco's shoe shine stand with two brushes and rag
"You're Never Alone With An Ego" (Book) preset in shoe shine box
Moony's flask
Typewriter on table with typed paper ("A little songbird . . .") for Dolly
Large newspaper in bag for Newsboy "Maxwell Chesterfield suicide
Three boxes of dead roses and white telephone preset on piano
Press Clipping for Dolly ("Rumor Hath It . . .")
Press clipping for Dolly ("October 14, 1934. Boo-hoo.")
Notebook for Moony
Trumpet for Actor 1
Silver tray w/bottle of cognac, 2 small glasses, waiter's napkin, 2 beer mats
Makeup for NAZI PARTY POOPER on piano
Press camera
Press clipping for Dolly ("Which socialist socialite")
Envelope w/wad of bills for Moony
Green checked tablecloth

2-New York "Times" for Newsboy ("Stop press. Hollywood columnist") & Moony
Writing case for Bella with fountain pen
Fake U.S. rifle (Marlene)
Oscar stand with Oscars preset on piano
Table and two chairs
Lamppost for "Girl in the Window"

ACT TWO

Stage Left

Table and chair preset down left with ashtray, old butts, manuscripts, cigarettes, matches, pencil sharpener, and mug w/pencils (no erasers)
Axe for "Happy Hickory"
CLIMBIN' music for Bonny
Stopwatch for Alvin Burns
Keys in case for Actor 1
Moscow radio transcript ("Soviet troops . . .")
Variety clipping (Shapiro-pinko-stinko")
Guitar for Bob Dylan and live mike
Drum wagon w/snare drum, bass drum, small tom-tom, large tom-tom, two cymbals and a high hat
Bella's letter and pen preset on table — (Writing case)
Open bottle of Johnny Walker w/glass
"Moon In June" (Book)
DON'T PLAY THAT LOVESONG manuscript for Storyteller
Straw hat for NOSTALGIA

Stage Right

Piano with glass ashtray off right
Letter from Oscar Hammerstein in frame
Three gift wrapped boxes
London *Daily Sketch* (May 5, 1960 "Moony Happy Hickory" Shapiro) for Actor 1
Acoustic guitar
Harmonica in holder (key of D)
One rolled joint
Dark sunglasses

Gold watch for Tilly
Guitar for Actress 2
Guitar for Actress 1 and live mike
Daily Express for Actor 1 (March 10, 1979 "Mrs. Moony Shapiro)
Six letters present on piano
  1. Bella
  2. Magda
  3. Lee
  4. Bella
  5. Bonny
  6. Bella
Crate of Johnny Walker preset under piano
Cigarette, lighter and ashtray preset on piano
Irish Times for Bella "Sheila O'Toole"
Gold watch for Storyteller
Two gold watches for Moony
Cane for NOSTALGIA
Cane for Moony
Korean lamp
On piano: candelabra, silver frames w/photos, rose vase

www.ingramcontent.com/pod-product-compliance
Lightning Source LLC
Chambersburg PA
CBHW072018290426
44109CB00018B/2274